Pilgrim Walk IN THE WOODS

SUSANNE HASSELL PHOTOGRAPHS BY PAUL HASSELL

Published by Vision Run Publishing
305 Portsmouth Rd. • Knoxville TN 37909
www.VisionRun.com

ISBN 978-0-9826098-9-7

Printed in the United States.
Printed on recycled paper.

Photography by Paul Hassell, www.PaulHassell.com

Design by Deb Hardison, www.DebHardison.com

DEDICATION

We dedicate this book to Jonathan David Hassell, beloved son and brother.

May God's path fill you with joy!

YOU SHOW ME
THE PATH OF
LIFE, IN YOUR
PRESENCE THERE
IS FULLNESS OF
JOY...

PS. 16:11 (NRSV)

ACKNOWLEDGEMENTS

We are grateful to all our walking companions and innumerable friends who continue to support us on our journeys. Many have helped to birth this book and we are especially thankful for these supportive midwives:

Debbie Patrick and Barbara Jones, patient publishers at Vision Run

Deb Hardison, gifted graphic designer

Austin Church, wise editor

Wendy Masters and Angela Gonda, who tracked down copyright permissions

The Fellows, who proofread the book

Carol Cline Ottaviano, who promoted the book long before it was a reality

Rose Echols, Susanne's fellow pilgrim in Iona.

Thanks to the many authors who shared their wisdom in the pages of this book.

INVITATION

NO WRITING ON
THE SOLITARY
MEDITATIVE
DIMENSIONS OF
LIFE CAN SAY
ANYTHING THAT
HAS NOT ALREADY
BEEN SAID BETTER
BY THE WIND IN
THE PINES.

THOMAS MERTON

On a pilgrimage to the Iona community, off the coast of Scotland, I was invited to take a day-long Pilgrim Walk around the island. That became one of the most special days of my life: hiking outdoors with new friends from around the world, reading poetry and scripture, and learning songs and history about the islanders. I couldn't sleep that night but lay awake anticipating my return home to East Tennessee and the prospect of leading others on Pilgrim Walks in the Great Smoky Mountains that are so dear to me.

As a retreat leader, I began to offer afternoon contemplative walks and soon discovered that they became the high point of retreats. Some people confided that the walk was the first time they had ever "really prayed." Prayer is an intimate conversation, speaking and listening to the One who loves us, but many have difficulty sitting in meditation. Quiet walking and attentive listening, however, enable us to pray in new ways as God speaks in the silence and in the music of creation.

We learn to pray with our heads bowed, hands folded, and eyes closed. Though this posture shows reverence and helps us to focus on God, there are other ways to pray. Try praying today with your eyes, ears, and heart wide open. Absorb the colorful beauty before you. Hear the "sounds of silence" in nature. Feel the wind and textures of the earth. Smell the aromas that surround you.

We are all "pilgrims," and this way of praying enriches the journey of life. Most religions consider pilgrimage a significant spiritual discipline, much different from a trip undertaken by a tourist or ordinary traveler. Pilgrimage involves risk and possibility. It invites change and conversion. The pilgrim may return as a different person. A pilgrimage may mean a long journey, but one can happen anywhere—even here in the woods!

Pilgrimages spring from a deep yearning to encounter God. This yearning draws us as pilgrims to special times and places where we cross the threshold of the unknown, enter a new dimension, walk into a liminal place. Ancient travelers did not set out on pilgrimage flippantly. They understood that encounters with the unknown could change them, and such changes are daunting.

Early Christian Celts described special places where they encountered God as "thin places." Only a thin veil separated the seen and the unseen, the natural world and the holy, the finite and the infinite, the physical and the spiritual realms. Be attentive to your own "thin places" as you walk this journey. St. Augustine said, "God is everywhere, it is true, and He that made all things is not contained or confined to dwell in any place."

I offer this book as a field guide for your spiritual journey outdoors. Don't let it gather dust on your coffee table or nightstand. Use it. To experience God in nature, you must *be* in nature. If you cannot walk or have no access to woods or a backyard or park, I hope that the photographs provided with each meditation will aid in your reflections.

CLIMB THE MOUNTAINS AND GET THE GOOD TIDINGS. NATURE'S PEACE WILL FLOW INTO YOU AS SUNSHINE FLOWS INTO TREES. THE WINDS WILL BLOW THEIR FRESHNESS INTO YOU, AND THE STORMS THEIR ENERGY, WHILE CARES WILL DROP OFF AS AUTUMN LEAVES.

JOHN MUIR

TIPS FOR THE JOURNEY

Pay attention. Be open to mystery.

Travel lightly with few possessions. Less is more.

Carry a journal and stop often to reflect. Jot down impressions, thoughts, feelings, and discoveries.

Immerse your journey in prayer. Speak and listen to God.

Be mindful—fully present. Let go of your worries, unfinished tasks, and responsibilities for awhile. Too often, we focus on the past or the future. Receive the gift of Now. Thich Nhat Hanh recommends walking with no particular aim, just for the sake of walking. He instructs pilgrims to be aware of their breathing, not controlling it, but counting inhales and exhales as a means of mindful meditation.

Walk leisurely, at a pace that suits you. The goal is not to "finish" the path, but to absorb the wonders of God that are before you.

Return with a tangible memento as a reminder of your experience: a rock, flower, feather, photograph, or poem; something that will remind you in the days ahead of what you have seen and heard.

If you are walking with a group, focus your eyes on the beauty around you, not on the reader. The guide can stop anywhere along the path to read or pray, using the Index to locate appropriate reflections, but all pilgrim walkers should feel the freedom to stop the group when they encounter something of interest. If you must use words while you walk, speak softly. Express gratitude for all you experience.

Be gentle with yourself. Slow down. Rest. Be still and know God.

The journey continues...

> Bless to us, O God,
> the earth beneath our feet.
> Bless to us, O God,
> the path whereon we go.
> Bless to us, O God,
> the people whom we meet.
>
> *Celtic Prayer*

SUSANNE HASSELL

S usanne is founder and director of Holy Paths, Inc. She has years of experience walking with people on their faith journeys as a spiritual director and retreat leader.

She received a Masters in Child and Family Studies from the University of Tennessee and founded three preschools before completing the Certificate of Spiritual Formation at Columbia Theological Seminary in Atlanta, and a Diploma in the Art of Spiritual Direction from San Francisco Theological Seminary. She will complete her Doctor of Ministry at SFTS in 2012.

Susanne is the mother of three grown children in Knoxville, Tennessee, Jonathan, Sarah, and Paul. The Hassell family is committed to offering hospitality and fostering unity, cooperation, and love within the church community and others who seek to know God. The family has spent countless days hiking and camping in the woods, especially in the Great Smoky Mountains near their home.

PAUL HASSELL

Paul Hassell is based in Knoxville, Tennessee near the foothills of the Great Smoky Mountains. He travels to breathtaking lands around the world, but the Smokies always call him home. Paul has a contagious love for life, adventure, and celebrating light. He graduated from the University of Tennessee in May 2008 with a customized major in Freelance Photography and Writing for the Natural Environment.

Paul frequently shows his fine art photographs in prestigious galleries. His adventure stories are published in local newspaper and his images have appeared in *National Parks* and other national magazines.

Paul is a member of the North American Nature Photography Association and Southern Appalachian Nature Photographers.

"When we find what really makes us tick, we must pursue it and let nothing keep us from that pursuit. From the age of 11 it's been quite clear that adventures and light are what make me tick. I've not ceased chasing the light ever since."
—Paul Hassell

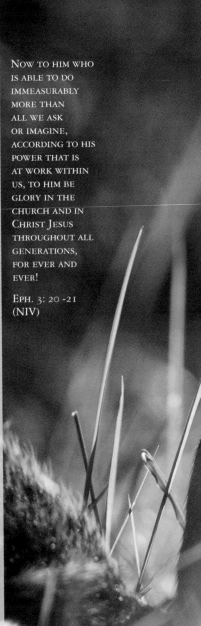

I pluck an acorn and hold it to my ear, and this is what it says to me: "By and by the birds will come and nest in me.

By and by, I will furnish shade for the cattle.

By and by I will provide warmth for the home.

By and by I will be shelter from the storm to those who have gone under the roof.

By and by I will be the strong ribs of a great vessel, and the tempest will beat against me in vain, while I carry men across the Atlantic."

"O foolish little acorn, wilt thou be all this?" I ask.

And the acorn answers, "Yes, God and I."

—*Lyman Abbott*

In what ways are you limiting yourself and what God can do in your life?

Do you believe that God has a good plan for your future?

ALL THINGS BRIGHT
AND BEAUTIFUL

Sing or recite this old hymn as you gaze at the wonders around you, praying for "eyes to see them, and lips that we might tell."

All things bright and beautiful,
all creatures great and small,
all things wise and wonderful:
the Lord God made them all.

Each little flower that opens,
each little bird that sings,
God made their glowing colors,
and made their tiny wings.

The purple-headed mountains,
the river running by,
the sunset and the morning
that brightens up the sky.

The cold wind in the winter,
the pleasant summer sun,
the ripe fruits in the garden:
God made them every one.

God gave us eyes to see them,
and lips that we might tell
how great is God Almighty,
who has made all things well.

—*Cecil F. Alexander*

B ut ask the animals, and they will teach you;
the birds of the air, and they will tell you;
ask the plants of the earth, and they will teach you;
and the fish of the sea will declare to you.
Who among all these does not know
that the hand of the Lord has done this?
In his hand is the life of every living thing
and the breath of every human being.

Then the Lord answered Job out of the whirlwind:

"Where were you when I laid the foundation of the earth?
Tell me, if you have understanding.
Who determined its measurements – surely you know!
Or who stretched the line upon it?
On what were its bases sunk,
or who laid its cornerstone
when the morning stars sang together
and all the heavenly beings shouted for joy?"

JOB 12:7-10, 38:1, 4-7 (NRSV)

*What is nature
teaching you about
God's character for
creation and plans
for your life?*

*What would need
to change in your
life for it
to become God-
centered?*

Father Damien
of the Abbey of
Gethsemani says
that we can only
know Creator
God to the degree
that we recognize
ourselves as the
creature. In other
words, if you
remain the center
of your universe,
you leave no room
for God.

Like Job, we are
called in humility
to recognize God
alone as the center
of creation and to
plead ignorance
about God's plans
for creation. But
piety doesn't earn
us freedom from
suffering. God
does what he
pleases. Without
answering Job's
or your questions
about suffering
or divine justice,
God affirms God's
goodness and
sovereignty.

In what ways are you feeling anxious today?

Be still and watch the birds. Listen. What do they have to say about entrusting God with your cares and worries?

S aid the Robin to the Sparrow,
"I should really like to know,
why these anxious human
beings run around and worry so."

Said the Sparrow to the Robin,
"Friend, I think that it must be
that they have no Heavenly Father
such as cares for you
and me."

—*Annie Elizabeth Cheney*

LOOK AT THE
BIRDS OF THE AIR;
THEY NEITHER
SOW NOR REAP
NOR GATHER
INTO BARNS,
AND YET YOUR
HEAVENLY
FATHER FEEDS
THEM.
ARE YOU NOT
OF MORE VALUE
THAN THEY?

MATT. 6:26
(NRSV)

CAST ALL YOUR
ANXIETY ON
[GOD], BECAUSE
HE CARES FOR
YOU.

I PETER 5:7
(NRSV)

Perhaps in God's ears, all of this world's sounds really are songs of praise – and what a chorus it is! Some time ago an ornithologist observed a single red-eyed vireo singing its song 22,197 times in a single day! Conservative estimates say that in North America alone there are as many as six billion land birds. So let us be conservative and say that on a given day in the season of spring – the time of the year when birds tend to sing the most – each of these birds sings its song about 10,000 times. That would be, in North America alone, sixty trillion songs in just one day. "Day after day they pour forth speech." Indeed they do, and God is listening.

—*Scott Hoezee*

Sit awhile and listen for bird calls. What do their songs say about God?

What is your song? How can you sing praises to God today?

EVEN THE SPARROW HAS FOUND A HOME,
 AND THE SWALLOW A NEST FOR HERSELF,
 WHERE SHE MAY HAVE HER YOUNG —
A PLACE NEAR YOUR ALTAR.
 O LORD ALMIGHTY, MY KING AND MY GOD.

Ps. 84:3 (NIV)

QUIT YOUR
FLAPPING AND
RIDE THE
THERMALS.
LEARN HOW
TO SOAR.

DEWITT JONES

If the wings are held outstretched without motion there will be an uplift if the air is full of little motions, swirls and quiverings. The wonderful gliding of birds that travel for miles without a movement of the wings or any apparent effort may conceivably be connected with this effect; it is said that it does not take place when the air is perfectly still.

— *Sir William Bragg*

What would it be like to soar
and catch the thermals?

As you marvel at birds soaring
across the sky, imagine embracing the
"motions, swirls, and quiverings"
of your life as God's way of providing
a quiet, peaceful spirit.

Although a bird or animal may protect its territory, it doesn't seek to own it.

It doesn't post a "no trespassing" sign.

How could you share more generously with others?

When a male bird – a vireo, for example – sings his belligerent song at another male vireo that approaches his neck of the woods, he is singing about family. It's a little bit like grumbling over the handsome delivery person who's getting too friendly with your spouse…and nothing at all like a no trespassing sign. The vireo doesn't waste his breath on the groundhogs gathering chestnuts under his nose, or the walnut trees using the sunlight to make their food, the grubs churning leaves into soil, the browsing deer, or even other birds that come to glean seeds that are useless to a vireo's children…This is the marvelous construct of "niche," the very particular way an organism uses its habitat, and it allows for an almost incomprehensible degree of peaceful coexistence.

Choose a cubic foot of earth, about anywhere that isn't paved; look closely enough, and you'll find that thousands of different kinds of living things are sharing that place, each one merrily surviving on something its neighbors couldn't use for all the tea in China. I'm told that nine-tenths of human law is about possession. But it seems to me we don't know the first thing about it.

—*Barbara Kingsolver*

Tiny green buds on a barren branch remind us of the promise of new birth. If we could peek inside a bud, we would discover tightly folded leaves, some lengthwise and others rolled from both sides to the center like a scroll.

Each leaf's perfect folds protect the center vein which carries nourishment. Each new leaf's potential lies curled within the branch, waiting for light and warmth. Spring will cause it to unfurl and expand into shade or a fragrant bloom.

We are buds, waiting to expand and discover the special gifts God has promised to us. When we open ourselves to God's light, God causes us to grow and develop into the unique beings we are created to be. We blossom in unforeseen ways!

I ask that your minds may be opened to see [God's] light, so that you will know what is the hope to which he has called you, how rich are the wonderful blessings he promises his people, and how very great is his power at work in us who believe.

Eph. 1:18-19 (GNT)

*How is God
inviting you to
become a new
creation?*

*What needs to
happen for you
to "open to God's
light"?*

God works best in the darkness. The ugly caterpillar in its shriveled cocoon sees nothing but days and weeks of darkness. Yet, God works a miracle in the midst of that darkness. John of the Cross calls this the "dark night of the soul." The butterfly in the chrysalis, baby in the mother's womb, seed in the ground, and authentic self in the soul must all pass a season in darkness.

In scriptures, Jonah emerged from the dark belly of the whale, Joseph escaped the dark pit where he'd been left to die, Paul was rescued from the dark prison cell, and Jesus rose from the grave. All passed through darkness into transformation—a new understanding and appreciation of themselves, their mission in life, and the mystery of God.

I WILL GIVE YOU THE TREASURES OF DARKNESS, RICHES STORED IN SECRET PLACES, SO THAT YOU MAY KNOW THAT I AM THE LORD, THE GOD OF ISRAEL, WHO SUMMONS YOU BY NAME.

Is. 45:3 (NIV)

What darkness pervades your life right now?

Can you discern how God is working in your life, even if you can't see it?

Can you identify any treasures of darkness God has given to sustain you?

I never wanted to be born.

The older I grew,
the fonder I became
of my mother's womb
and its warmth and its safety.

I feared the unknown:
            the next world,
about which I knew nothing
but imagined the worst.

Yet, as I grew older,
I sensed in my soul
that the womb was not my
home forever.

Though I did not know when,
I felt that one day
I would disappear through a door
which had yet to be opened,
and confront the unknown
of which I was afraid.

And then,
it happened.

In blood, tears and pain,
it happened.

I was cut off from the familiar;
I left my life behind
and discovered not darkness but light,

not hostility, but love,
not eternal separation
but hands that wanted to hold me.

I never wanted to be born.

I don't want to die.

The older I grow,
the fonder I become
of this world
and its warmth and its safety.

I fear the unknown;
            the next world,
about which I know nothing
but imagine the worst.

Yet, as I grow older,
I sense in my soul
that this world is not my
home forever.
Though I do not know when,
I feel that one day
I will disappear through a door
which has yet to be opened,

Perhaps having come so safely
through the first door,
I should not fear so hopelessly the
second.

— *John Bell*

*What are your
honest feelings
about death?
Acknowledge
your fears and
doubts and pay
attention to God's
message of hope
and promise.*

Despite all our talk about the sun rising and setting, it never moves. It never changes. By contrast, we humans move, shift, and realign constantly. We resemble clouds.

Clouds are the tool that God uses to reveal new facets of the sun. Clouds give the sun its many textures, shapes, and colors, and without clouds, sunsets are unremarkable. Notice how the darkest storm clouds transform when sunlight strikes them. They reveal explosions of lemon, tangerine, lavender, and ruby. We celebrate sunsets for their stunning beauty, yet our appreciation and knowledge of the sun's character draw strength from unglamorous helpers—clouds.

The abundance and texture of the clouds around us deepen our fascination with the sun. Look for them. Wait upon the sunlight to spread their paints across the deep azure.

—Paul Hassell

What clouds in your life present themselves as a means for you to develop a greater adoration for God who shines through them?

As you gaze at
this crossroad,
imagine the
choices before you.

Which way will
you choose? If
you're not sure,
God invites
you, "Ask," and
Jesus bids you,
"Come."

This is what the Lord says: "Stand at the crossroads and look; ask for the ancient paths, ask where the good way is, and walk in it, and you will find rest for your souls."

Jer. 6:16 (NIV)

When we come to forks in the road, we must make a choice. God tells us to choose the tried and true way of our righteous Hebrew ancestors. If we commit to God's path—if we "walk in it"—we will receive "rest for our souls."

Jesus offers the same promise: "Come to me, all you who are weary and burdened, and I will give you rest. Take my yoke upon you and learn from me, for I am gentle and humble in heart, and you will find rest for your souls. For my yoke is easy and my burden is light."

Matt. 11: 28-29 (NIV)

What is cluttering your "nest"?
What do you need to let go of in order
to make space for God?

Our minds are like crows. They pick up everything that glitters, no matter how uncomfortable our nests get with all that metal in them.

—*Thomas Merton*

St. Augustine said that God is always trying to give good things to us, but our hands are too full to receive them. Clutch your fists tightly and imagine the impossibility of receiving a gift. In the same way, we cling to things that will never satisfy our deepest longings: food, money, technology, sports, charitable activites, relationships. Even good things can clutter our lives and prevent us from receiving God's best gifts. And it is not only physical possessions that clutter our attention and time; our hearts and thoughts are also filled with distractions that occupy space where God might dwell.

Let us remain as empty as possible so that God can fill us up.

—*Mother Teresa*

A commonplace life, we say, and we sigh.
But why should we sigh as we say?

The commonplace sun in the commonplace sky
Makes up the commonplace day;
The moon and the stars are commonplace things,
And the flower that blooms, and the bird that sings;
But dark were the world, and sad our lot,
If the flowers failed, and the sun shone not;
And God, who studies each separate soul,
Out of commonplace lives makes His beautiful whole.

—Susan Coolidge

How have you dismissed your life as "commonplace" or ordinary?

As you gaze at nature around you, take time to appreciate how extraordinary you are!

A

All people are grass,

their constancy is like the

flower of the field,

The grass withers, the

flower fades, when the breath

of the Lord blows upon it;

surely the people are grass.

The grass withers, the

flower fades; but the word of

our God will stand forever.

ISAIAH 40: 6-8 (NRSV)

As you walk,
pick a dry blade
of grass and
remember a time
when your faith
felt dry and
barren.

How, when and
where do you find
life-giving "water"
for your soul?

Pay attention to any life practices that come to mind as you walk.

In what ways might your personal indulgences be "spoiling the earth?"

Continue your walk, but walk slowly.
Step softly.
Recite one of the poems as you walk.

What does it mean to "enjoy the earth gently?"

For centuries, far too many Christians have presumed that God's love is primarily directed at them, and that his natural order was created mainly for the use, and abuse, of humankind. Today such a human-centered attitude to our fragile and exhausted planet is at last beginning to look not only selfish and parochial, but also irresponsible and potentially dangerous. Hence all of us must open our eyes and minds wider still. We must realize that the way to maintain the value and preciousness of the human is by reaffirming the preciousness of the non-human also - of all that is. Indeed, the Christian God forbids the idea of a cheap creation, of a finite, disposable universe. God's universe is a work of non-expendable and ever-renewing love - and nothing that is fashioned in love must ever be regarded as cheap or secondary.

—*Robert Runcie*

Teach us, Lord, to walk the soft earth as relatives of all that live.

—*Native American Prayer*

Enjoy the earth gently,
Enjoy the earth gently;
For if the earth is spoiled
it cannot be repaired.
Enjoy the earth gently.

—*Yoruba poem, West Africa*

WHAT, AFTER ALL, IS APOLLOS? AND WHAT IS PAUL? ONLY SERVANTS, THROUGH WHOM YOU CAME TO BELIEVE – AS THE LORD HAS ASSIGNED TO EACH HIS TASK. I PLANTED THE SEED, APOLLOS WATERED IT, BUT GOD MADE IT GROW. SO NEITHER HE WHO PLANTS NOR HE WHO WATERS IS ANYTHING, BUT ONLY GOD WHO MAKES THINGS GROW. THE ONE WHO PLANTS AND THE ONE WHO WATERS HAVE ONE PURPOSE, AND EACH WILL BE REWARDED ACCORDING TO HIS OWN LABOR. FOR WE ARE GOD'S FELLOW WORKERS; YOU ARE GOD'S FIELD, GOD'S BUILDING.

I COR. 3:5-9 (NIV)

…I TELL YOU, LOOK AROUND YOU, AND SEE HOW THE FIELDS ARE RIPE FOR HARVESTING. THE REAPER IS ALREADY RECEIVING WAGES AND IS GATHERING FRUIT FOR ETERNAL LIFE, SO THAT SOWER AND REAPER MAY REJOICE TOGETHER. FOR HERE THE SAYING HOLDS TRUE, 'ONE SOWS AND ANOTHER REAPS.' I SENT YOU TO REAP THAT FOR WHICH YOU DID NOT LABOUR. OTHERS HAVE LABOURED, AND YOU HAVE ENTERED INTO THEIR LABOUR.

JOHN 4:35B-38 (NRSV)

JESUS SAID TO HIS DISCIPLES, "THE HARVEST IS PLENTIFUL BUT THE LABOURERS ARE FEW; THEREFORE ASK THE LORD OF THE HARVEST TO SEND OUT LABOURERS INTO HIS HARVEST FIELD."

MATT. 9:37-38 (NRSV)

How might God be calling you to plant, water, sow, or reap?

When fire breaks loose and rages on its own account, it carries swift destruction in its course; but, when restricted within certain bounds, it warms our rooms and cooks our food, illuminates our towns and drives our locomotives.

In the same way, water, when in flood, roots up trees, carries away houses, and sweeps the crops from the fields; but, when confined within its banks, drives the wheel and floats the barge and rejoices the eye…

So the very qualities that, when unregulated, waste and brutalize life may, when subjected to the control of temperance, be its fairest ornaments.

—James Stalker

What is one thing in your life that can easily get out of control, resulting in waste and brutality?

Establishing boundaries is the virtue of temperance. How can they release you for beauty and purpose?

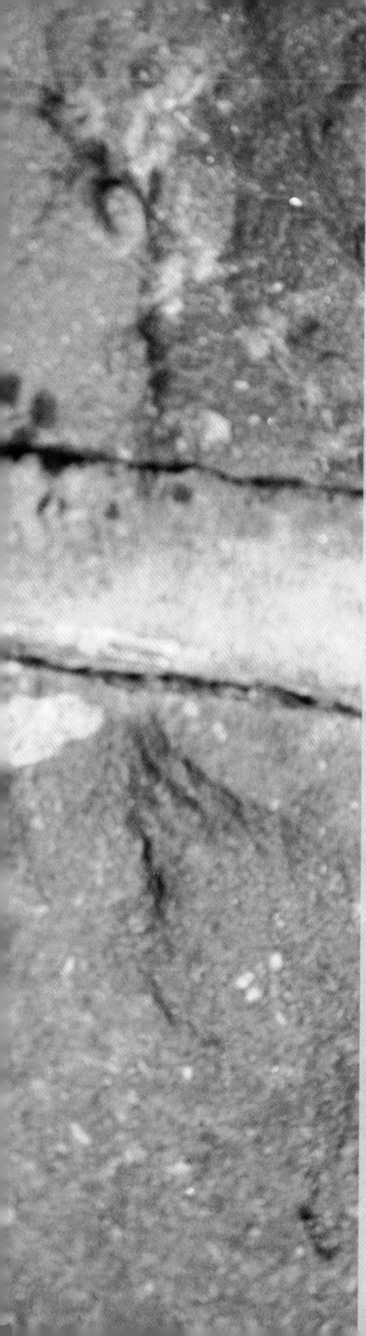

Flower in the crannied wall,
  I pluck you out of the crannies,
  I hold you here, root and all,
  in my hand,
Little flower – but if I could understand
What you are, root and all, and all in all,
I should know what God and man is.

—*Alfred Lord Tennyson*

*How long has it
been since you
were awe-struck at
discovering something
so insignificant as a
small flower growing
out of a crack in a
wall or sidewalk?*

*What might you
be missing as you
scurry past all sorts
of extraordinary, if
quiet, spectacles in
nature?*

*How might you
cultivate childlike
wonder?*

Fat buds on the trees and spring daffodils just beginning to bloom behind a rock at the bottom of a deep ravine promise new creation. They remind us of God's extravagance, creating flowers for God's eyes alone. When I came across them, I felt as though I was on holy ground. They will proclaim the glory of God until they wither and die, whether anybody sees them or not.

What they do unconsciously, you are called to do consciously—to be still, wait, trust, and grow into the beauty that is you; to proclaim God's creative and sustaining love. As you marvel at the hidden beauty of flowers and buds, God is saying, "Slow down. For you to simply be here with me is enough."

Imagine that God has created all that is before you just for You! You are God's Beloved, worthy of God's extravagant gifts.

Thank the God "who is able to do immeasurably more than all we ask or imagine" for blessing you from God's generous abundance. (Eph. 3:20)

What kind of bouquet will you present to God at the end of this walk, day, or week?

How well do you receive compliments or affirmations? What is your response when you hear "well done" or "good job"? Corrie Ten Boom was arrested for sheltering Jews in Holland and imprisoned in the German concentration camp, Ravensbruck. All her family died, but Corrie was finally released and spent the next thirty-three years traveling the world to share her simple Gospel message of God's love and forgiveness.

Corrie became famous and touched hundreds of lives through her book, *The Hiding Place.* Yet, those who knew her say that she never became boastful or proud when she received international acclaim. Neither was she reluctant to receive praises from her admirers. She once explained that her way of handling compliments was to take each one as a flower, then gather them together in a bouquet and present them to Jesus, "Here, Lord Jesus, these belong to You."

Who are the "frogs" in your life who need a kiss?

Y ou ever feel like a frog? Frogs feel slow, low, puffy, ugly, drooped, pooped. I know. One told me. Frog feeling comes when you want to be bright but feel dumb, when you want to share but are selfish, when you want to be thankful but feel resentful, when you want to be great but are small, when you want to care but are indifferent. Yes, at one time or another each of us has found himself on a lily pad floating down the great river of life. Frightened and disgusted, we are too froggish to budge.

Once upon a time there was a frog but he really wasn't a frog. He was a prince who looked and felt like a frog. A wicked witch had cast a spell on him and only the kiss of a beautiful maiden could save him. But since when do cute chicks kiss frogs? So there he sat, unkissed prince in frog form. But miracles do happen and one day a beautiful maiden grabbed him up and gave him a big smack. Crash, boom, zap! There he was, a handsome prince...

—Bruce Larson

In this fairy tale, we see the task of the Church—to kiss frogs. Jesus called a motley crew of "frogs" to be his disciples. None of them had any outstanding talents or abilities, but Jesus took those unlikely prospects and invited them to follow. They responded by dropping their nets, walking away from their tedious routines, and becoming transformed into new and significant men in the process.

You are here today because someone at sometime loved you, warts and all. A teacher, parent, friend, or even stranger accepted and cared about you and shared God's love, enabling you to become the beautiful creature you were created to be. Though you may still have plenty of warts, your job is to kiss more frogs, just as God kissed you through another person.

Jesus was hungry. Seeing in the distance a fig tree in leaf, he went to find out if it had any fruit. When he reached it, he found nothing but leaves, because it was not the season for figs. Then he said to the tree, "May no one ever eat fruit from you again."

[The next] morning, as they went along, they saw the fig tree withered from the roots. Peter remembered and said to Jesus, "Rabbi, look! The fig tree you cursed has withered!"

Mark 11:12-14, 20-21 (NIV)

A fig tree full of leaves should bear fruit. More than once, Jesus uses fruit trees as an analogy to illustrate how the Pharisees appear to be holy and righteous but don't live faithful lives of charity and compassion.

Our actions should mirror what we profess we believe. If you consider yourself generous, do your checkbook and calendar reflect that? If you value hospitality, do you open your heart, home, and life to family, friends, and strangers? If you profess to be a person of prayer, does your inner life substantiate that claim?

God created trees and human beings to bear fruit. If you fail to produce the fruit, then the Great Arborist may prune you to make room for faithful fruit-bearers.

The fruit of the Spirit is love, joy, peace, patience, kindness, goodness, faithfulness, gentleness, and self-control.

Gal. 5:22-23 (NIV)

*Reflect honestly on
your life. What
fruit do you see?*

*Are you withered
and dry or are you
bearing the fruit of
God's Spirit?*

Geese in a flock have 70% greater range than a lone goose, and geese in formation fly 75% faster than a goose flying alone.

Geese remind us that we function better within communities. If we live only for ourselves, we are incomplete and ineffective. Like the geese, we are dependent upon one another, sometimes for necessities and physical needs, but always for emotional and spiritual strength expressed through sharing.

The body of Christ is such a community of faith.

THE BODY IS A UNIT, THOUGH IT IS MADE UP OF MANY PARTS; AND THOUGH ALL ITS PARTS ARE MANY, THEY FORM ONE BODY. SO IT IS WITH CHRIST...THE EYE CANNOT SAY TO THE HAND, "I DON'T NEED YOU!" ...GOD HAS COMBINED THE MEMBERS OF THE BODY...SO THAT THERE SHOULD BE NO DIVISION IN THE BODY, BUT THAT ITS PARTS SHOULD HAVE EQUAL CONCERN FOR EACH OTHER.

IF ONE PART SUFFERS, EVERY PART SUFFERS WITH IT; IF ONE PART IS HONORED, EVERY PART REJOICES WITH IT. NOW YOU ARE THE BODY OF CHRIST, AND EACH ONE OF YOU IS A PART OF IT.

1 COR. 12:12, 21, 24-27 (NIV)

How might God be calling you to help form or support a more intentional community in your home, church, or workplace?

Prayer of Seven Directions

With beauty before me,
    May I walk
With beauty behind me,
    May I walk
With beauty on my right,
    May I walk
With beauty on my left,
    May I walk
With beauty above me,
    May I walk
With beauty below me,
    May I walk
With beauty inside me,
    May I walk
Wandering on a trail of beauty,
    Lively, I walk

—Adapted from a Navajo prayer

*As you recite this, pray with your body. Stretch your arms
before, behind, to the right and left, above, below, inside
(touching your chest) and wandering (opening your hands like
a blossom outward.)*

Christ be with me, Christ within me,
Christ behind me, Christ before me,
Christ beside me, Christ to win me,
Christ to comfort and restore me.
Christ beneath me, Christ above me,
Christ in quiet, Christ in danger,
Christ in hearts of all that love me,
Christ in mouth of friend and stranger.

—St. Patrick's Breastplate Prayer

GOD'S GRANDEUR

The world is charged with the grandeur of God.
   It will flame out, like shining from shook foil;
It gathers to a greatness, like the ooze of oil
Crushed. Why do men then now not reck his rod?
Generations have trod, have trod, have trod;
And all is seared with trade; Bleared, smeared with toil;
And wears man's smudge and shares man's smell: the soil
Is bare now, nor can foot feel, being shod.

And for all this, nature is never spent;
There lives the dearest freshness deep down things;
And though the last lights off the black West went
Oh, morning, at the brown brink eastward, springs –
Because the Holy Ghost over the bent
World broods with warm breast and with ah! bright wings.

—*Gerard Manley Hopkins*

Where have you experienced God's grandeur?

When have you, like the poet, been moved so deeply by God's freshness in "deep down things" that you had a hard time expressing how you felt?

O Lord, our Sovereign, how majestic is your name in all the earth!

When I look at your heavens, the
work of your fingers,
the moon and the stars that you
have established;
what are human beings that you
are mindful of them,
mortals that you care for them?

Yet you have made them a little
lower than God,
and crowned them with glory
and honor.
You have given them dominion
over the works of your hands;
you have put all things under their
feet, all sheep and oxen,
and also the beasts of the field,
the birds of the air, and the fish
of the sea...

O Lord, our Sovereign, how majestic
is your name in all the earth!

Ps. 8, SELECTED VERSES (NRSV)

THIS IS THE
DAY THAT THE
LORD HAS
MADE, LET US
REJOICE AND BE
GLAD IN IT.

Ps. 118:24
(NRSV)

Express gratitude for this day using a breath prayer as you walk.
For example:

Inhale...   God of Creation   Exhale...   I give you thanks.
              Divine Light...   show me the way.
              Lord Jesus...   have mercy on me.
              Spirit of Peace...   flow through me.

Nature photographer DeWitt Jones expresses his
life goal with these eight words:

> *Inhale: Take it all in...*
> *Exhale: Give it all back.*

I lift my eyes to the hills—where does my help come from?
My help comes from the Lord, the Maker of heaven and earth.
He will not let your foot slip—he who watches over you will not slumber;
indeed, he who watches over Israel will neither slumber nor sleep.
The Lord watches over you—the Lord is your shade at your right hand;
the sun will not harm you by day, nor the moon by night.
The Lord will keep you from all harm—he will watch over your life;
the Lord will watch over your coming and going, both now and forevermore.

Ps.121 (NIV)

This "psalm of ascent" was recited or sung as the Israelites made annual pilgrimage to Jerusalem and Mount Zion. Pilgrims were assured safe travel and unfailing protection, day and night, from the God of all creation.

What is the promise in this psalm for you today?

Have you flitted from one activity to another in the past few days? How might you be more intentional about spending time with God? What flowers has God provided for your nourishment and pleasure?

A hummingbird's wings beat sixty to seventy times a second. These miniature marvels can fly at speeds up to thirty-five miles per hour, hover in the same place, or fly sideways, up, down, forward, and even backward. Expending so much energy requires them to refuel often. With their long, pointed bills, they sip the nectar of hundreds of flowers every day. Yet, when they migrate south in the winter, they can fly five hundred miles without stopping.

I was gazing at one of these amazing creatures as it approached the feeder on my deck. It came close, hovered, then darted away to a nearby tree.

It soon zoomed in again, its wings humming, and hovered just out of reach of the life-giving sugar water that I provided. As I became frustrated with the tiny bird's hesitancy, I realized that it mirrored my own behavior toward God. How often I approach God, only to be diverted in another direction.

TASTE AND SEE THAT THE LORD IS GOOD; HAPPY ARE THOSE WHO TAKE REFUGE IN HIM.

O FEAR THE LORD, YOU HIS HOLY ONES, FOR THOSE WHO FEAR HIM HAVE NO WANT.

PS. 34:8-9 (NRSV)

Pay attention to anything that has crept into your life, threatening to invade your thought life, your home, or your relationships.

How is God challenging you to lay aside the "sin that so easily entangles" and restore wholeness and purity in your life?

Many non-native plant species enhance our gardens, but some of these, such as kudzu in the South, have invaded our woods and forests. With no indigenous insects or diseases to control its growth, kudzu has easily taken over the habitat of native plants. As such invasive species thrive, they compromise the diversity of our fragile ecosystem, affecting plants, wildlife and insects. We spend millions of dollars and years of labor trying to restore the balance. In a similar way, we welcome a habit, possession, or indulgence into our lives because it is attractive and, within proper boundaries, may be harmless. Sin and addictions, however, quickly take root in healthy things until we are entangled, consumed.

THEREFORE, SINCE WE ARE SURROUNDED BY SUCH A GREAT CLOUD OF WITNESSES, LET US THROW OFF EVERYTHING THAT HINDERS AND THE SIN THAT SO EASILY ENTANGLES, AND LET US RUN WITH PERSEVERANCE THE RACE MARKED OUT FOR US.

HEBREWS 12:1 (NIV)

What is this life if,
full of care,
We have no time to
stand and stare.
No time to stand beneath the boughs
And stare as long as sheep or cows.
No time to see, when woods we pass,
Where squirrels hide their
nuts in grass.
No time to see, in broad daylight,

Streams full of stars,
like skies at night.
No time to turn at Beauty's glance,
And watch her feet,
how they can dance.
No time to wait till her mouth can
Enrich that smile her eyes began.
A poor life this is if, full of care,
We have no time to stand and stare.

—*W. D. Davies*

God's glory is on tour in the skies,
  God-craft on exhibit across the horizon.
Madame Day holds classes every morning,
  Professor Night lectures each evening.

Their words aren't heard,
  their voices aren't recorded,
But their silence fills the earth:
  unspoken truth is spoken everywhere.

Ps. 19:1-4 (The Message)

Take time today to stand and stare often. Think of two or three ways to carve out more minutes each day to continue this practice.

Understand the creation if you wish to know the Creator…for those who wish to know the great deep must first review the natural world.

—St. Columbanus

Almighty God, Creator:
  The morning is yours, rising into fullness.
  The summer is yours, dipping into autumn.
Eternity is yours, dipping into time.
The vibrant grasses,
the scent of flowers,
the lichen on the rocks,
the tang of seaweed.
All is yours.
Gladly we live in this garden of your creating.

Celtic Prayer

The Celts came to know God through creation.

How are you living with gladness in this garden of God's creation?

The glory of the forest meadow is the lily…
After how many centuries of Nature's care planting and watering them, tucking the bulbs in snugly below winter's frost, shading the tender shoots with clouds drawn above them like curtains, pouring refreshing rain, making them perfect in beauty, and keeping them safe by a thousand miracles. So extravagant is Nature with her choicest treasures, spending plant beauty as she spends sunshine, pouring it forth into land and sea, garden and desert. And so the beauty of lilies falls on angels and men, bears and squirrels, wolves and sheep, birds and bees.

—*John Muir*

WHY DO YOU WORRY ABOUT
CLOTHING? CONSIDER THE LILIES OF
THE FIELD, HOW THEY GROW; THEY
NEITHER TOIL NOR SPIN, YET I TELL
YOU, EVEN SOLOMON IN ALL HIS
GLORY WAS NOT CLOTHED LIKE ONE
OF THESE.

MATT. 6:28-29 (NRSV)

*Marvel at the "thousand miracles"
God provides to keep the lilies alive and
beautiful.*

*Why is it so difficult to believe that God
will provide for you the same as these
short-lived lilies?*

ELIJAH TRAVELED FORTY DAYS AND FORTY NIGHTS UNTIL HE REACHED HOREB, THE MOUNTAIN OF GOD…

THE LORD SAID, "GO OUT AND STAND ON THE MOUNTAIN IN THE PRESENCE OF THE LORD, FOR THE LORD IS ABOUT TO PASS BY."

THEN A GREAT AND POWERFUL WIND TORE THE MOUNTAINS APART AND SHATTERED THE ROCKS BEFORE THE LORD, BUT THE LORD WAS NOT IN THE WIND.

AFTER THE WIND THERE WAS AN EARTHQUAKE, BUT THE LORD WAS NOT IN THE EARTHQUAKE.

AFTER THE EARTHQUAKE CAME A FIRE, BUT THE LORD WAS NOT IN THE FIRE. AND AFTER THE FIRE CAME A GENTLE WHISPER. WHEN ELIJAH

HEARD IT, HE PULLED HIS CLOAK OVER
HIS FACE AND WENT OUT AND STOOD
AT THE MOUTH OF THE CAVE.

I Kings 19:8-13 (NIV)

Like Elijah, I approach the mountain looking for God—for comfort in my sorrow, for justice in my anger, for hope in my despair, for answers to my questions...

Like Elijah, I must learn to wait patiently and to listen attentively. When the noisy storms move on, I recognize God in the gentle breeze...

Like Elijah, I discover what I was searching for and stand in reverence and awe...

Like Elijah...I will rise and return.

The soul should always stand ajar, ready to welcome the ecstatic experience.

—Emily Dickinson

What is God whispering today?

L ord, you set the mountains in place by your strength;
You calm the roar of the seas, and the noise of the waves;
The whole world stands in awe of your deeds,
of the great things you have done.
Your deeds bring shouts of joy from one end of the earth to the other
and every hillside declares your glory.

ADAPTED FROM PSALM 65

Just as clouds cloaked my view of the mountains, I often allow what I see in
the world to obscure my vision of what's real and forget that God is always
with me. God reveals the holy just enough to call me back, time and time
again.

Where is your focus?

What things in this world obscure your view of God's reality?

How can you be more aware of God who is unseen?

Holy mountains, you tease me this morning,
Taunting me with your peek-a-boo, and yet
You are the rocks, the faithful ones, abiding forever.
You are not hiding at all, You are not teasing me.

The mist, the clouds—they are the fickle ones.
Coming between us, obscuring you, as if they are what's real;
There you are again – only a glimpse, a reminder.
I long to see all of you, but a peek is enough for now.

—*Susanne V. Hassell*

We fix our eyes not on what is seen, but on what is unseen. For what is seen is temporary, but what is unseen is eternal.

II Cor. 4:18 (NIV)

On a walk one day I was feeling bogged down with troubles. As I waded through an enormous mud puddle, seeing it as an image of my life at that time, I spotted a heart right in the middle of the mud. God did not remove my difficulties, but with this simple sign, God, full of love and grace, promised to be with me in the midst of them.

The miracle is not to walk on water, or in thin air, but on the earth.

—*Thich Nhat Hanh*

I WAITED PATIENTLY FOR THE LORD;
HE TURNED TO ME AND HEARD MY CRY.
HE LIFTED ME OUT OF THE SLIMY PIT,
OUT OF THE MUD AND MIRE;
HE SET MY FEET ON A ROCK
AND GAVE ME A FIRM PLACE TO STAND.

PS. 40:1-2 (NIV)

How do you experience God's presence in the midst of pain or struggle?

How are you even now waiting for God to set your feet on a rock?

I think of life as a big wagon wheel with many spokes. In the middle is the hub. Often...it looks like we are running around the rim trying to reach everybody. But God says, "Start in the hub; live in the hub. Then you will be connected with all the spokes, and you won't have to run so fast."

— *Henri Nouwen*

Draw a wheel with spokes in the dirt or sand and consider the "spokes" in your life.

How might God be inviting you to live more "in the hub"?

Pray for open
eyes to see the
gifts of nature
today.

Pray for an
open heart to
absorb them.
Wait
patiently.

The rare moment is not the moment when there is something worth looking at, but the moment when we are capable of seeing.

—*Joseph Wood Krutch*

In the fields and woods more than anywhere else all things come to those who wait, because all things are on the move, and are sure sooner or later to come your way.

To absorb a thing is better than to learn it, and we absorb what we enjoy. We learn things at school, we absorb them in the fields and woods and on the farm. When we look upon Nature with fondness and appreciation she meets us halfway and takes a deeper hold upon us than when studiously conned. Hence I say the way of knowledge of Nature is the way of love and enjoyment, and is more surely found in the open air than in the school-room or the laboratory.

—*John Burroughs*

Often we are like Jacob when he said, "THE LORD IS IN THIS PLACE AND I DID NOT KNOW IT."

GENESIS 28:16 (NRSV)

Be aware of God's Presence today. Wonder about the impossibility of being anywhere in the universe where God is not present. God knows you completely and loves you just the same. There is nothing you can do to make God love you less; there is nothing you can do to make God love you more. How will you respond to such love?

Where might I go to find You,
Exalted, Hidden One?
Yet where would I not go to find You,
Everpresent, Eternal One?
My heart cries out to You:
Please draw near to me.
The moment I reach out for You,
I find You reaching in for me.

—*Hebrew Shabbat Evening Prayer*

LORD, you have searched me
and you know me. You know when I sit and
when I rise; you perceive my thoughts from afar.
You discern my going out and my lying down;
you are familiar with all my ways.
Before a word is on my tongue
you know it completely, O LORD.
You hem me in—behind and before;
you have laid your hand upon me.
Such knowledge is too wonderful for me,
too lofty for me to attain.
Where can I go from your Spirit?
Where can I flee from your presence?
If I go up to the heavens, you are there;
if I make my bed in the depths, you are there.
If I rise on the wings of the dawn,
if I settle on the far side of the sea,
even there your hand will guide me,
your right hand will hold me fast.
If I say, "Surely the darkness will hide me
and the light become night around me,"
even the darkness will not be dark to you;
the night will shine like the day,
for darkness is as light to you.

PSALM 139: 1-12 (NIV)

Hold a small nut in your palm and gaze at it.
What is God saying to you about God's love today?

God showed me something
small, no bigger than a
hazelnut,
lying in the palm of my hand,
    as it seemed to me,
and it was round as a ball.
I looked at it with the eye of my
understanding and thought:
What can this be?
I was amazed that it could last,
for I thought that because of its
littleness it would suddenly have
fallen into nothing.
And I was answered in my
understanding:
It lasts and always will, because
God loves it;
and thus everything has being
through the love of God.
God, of your goodness
give me yourself;
for you are sufficient for me.
I cannot properly ask anything less,
to be worthy of you.
If I were to ask less,
I should always be in want.
In you alone do I have all.

—*Julian of Norwich*

Julian understood three things:
God made it, God loves it,
God preserves it.

G rowing seems to be a common trait among living things. But I wonder
if anyone's ever done it better than an old pine.

If you're a pine, growth seems to have a lot to do with making the
best of where you get started. Sometimes that's just a bare-bones, blustery,
rocky outcrop of a place, inhospitable, with little soil or shelter, nurturing or
encouragement. It may take a long time, but you somehow come to grips with
it—this starting place. You reach and reach, stretching needy roots over naked
granite, through tiny cracks, down into crevices. Until you finally find the
footholds, the stability and sustenance you need. Then, someday, somehow,

you transcend…growing up, while at the same time growing down, and growing out. Growing through all kinds of disasters. Growing through them.

And that's all there is to it, it seems. Grow. Down. Out. Up. Don't stop. Just grow.

Simple enough. But maybe it's the hardest, most important thing in the world. Maybe everything depends on it. Maybe the whole world depends on it.

—Douglas Wood

Think of an area where you need to grow. Is this place a windy crag? Does it require special fortitude? What would it look like to come to grips with this place and make the best of it?

Mother Teresa of Calcutta prayed, "May God break my heart so completely that the whole world falls in." Not only Catholics, Americans, Indians, and righteous people, but the entire world! We are all created in the image of God, and God doesn't play favorites. Is it possible that God is calling each of us to embrace the whole world?

What would it take for you to pray Mother Teresa's prayer and feel brokenhearted for the suffering of people at your doorstep or around the world?

Who have you refused to let in?

Who are those who would "fall in" if God opened your heart completely? Those who have betrayed your trust? Those who lie and cheat? Those who abuse children, animals, or one another? Zealots driven by hatred and violence?

We want to make a difference in the world, to love others well, and to help provide the basic needs of those who are hungry, thirsty, lonely, or homeless. Dorothy Day assures us that "we can change the world: we can work for the oasis, the little cell of joy and peace in a harried world." Just as a pebble tossed into a pond makes ever-widening ripples, a life of mercy and justice influences those around us.

I WAS HUNGRY AND YOU GAVE ME FOOD, I WAS THIRSTY AND YOU GAVE ME SOMETHING TO DRINK, I WAS A STRANGER AND YOU WELCOMED ME, I WAS NAKED AND YOU GAVE ME CLOTHING, I WAS SICK AND YOU TOOK CARE OF ME, I WAS IN PRISON AND YOU VISITED ME. THEN THE RIGHTEOUS WILL ANSWER HIM, "LORD, WHEN WAS IT…?" AND [GOD] WILL ANSWER THEM, "TRULY I TELL YOU, JUST AS YOU DID IT TO ONE OF THE LEAST OF THESE…YOU DID IT TO ME."

MATT. 25: 35-36, 40 (NRSV)

How is God calling you to "change the world"?

Toss a pebble into the pond and imagine God touching others through your life.

May the blessing of light be on you,
Light without and light within.

May the blessed sunlight
Shine upon you and warm your heart till it glows
Like a great peat fire, so that the stranger may
Come and warm himself at it, as well as the friend.
And may the light shine out of the eyes of you,
Like a candle set in the windows of a house,
Bidding the wanderer to come in out of the storm.

And may the blessing of the rain
Be on you—the soft sweet rain.
May it fall upon your spirit so that all the little flowers
may spring up,
And shed their sweetness on the air.
And may the blessing of the great rains be on you,
That they beat upon your spirit and wash it
fair and clean,
And leave there many a shining pool where the blue
of the heaven shines,
and sometimes a star.

And may the blessing of the earth be on you
The great round earth;
May you ever have a kindly greeting
For people you pass as you are going along the roads.

And now may the Lord
Bless you, and bless you kindly.
Amen

—*Scottish Prayer*

Experience God's blessing raining down upon you.
Express your gratitude.

The poor and needy search for water, but there is none; their tongues are parched with thirst.

But I the Lord will answer them; I, the God of Israel, will not forsake them.

I will make rivers flow on barren heights, and springs within the valleys.

I will turn the desert into pools of water, and the parched ground into springs.

I will put in the desert the cedar and the acacia, the myrtle and the olive,

I will set pines in the wasteland, the fir and the cypress together, so that people may see and know, may consider and understand, that the hand of the Lord has done this.

Is. 41: 17-20 (NIV)

YOU WILL GO OUT IN JOY AND BE LED FORTH IN PEACE; THE MOUNTAINS AND HILLS WILL BURST INTO SONG BEFORE YOU, AND ALL THE TREES OF THE FIELD WILL CLAP THEIR HANDS. INSTEAD OF THE THORNBUSH WILL GROW THE PINE TREE, AND INSTEAD OF BRIERS THE MYRTLE WILL GROW.

Is. 55:12-13 (NIV)

How is God watering and renewing you this day?

Take a walk in the rain or snow and ask God to fill the dry and barren places within you.

Think of it: all that speech
pouring down, selling nothing,
judging nobody, drenching
the thick mulch of dead leaves,
soaking the trees, filling the gullies
and crannies of the wood with water,
washing out the places where men
have stripped the hillside! What a
thing it is to sit absolutely alone, in
the forest, at night, cherished by this
wonderful, unintelligible, perfectly
innocent speech, the most comforting
speech in the world, the talk that rain
makes by itself all over the ridges,
and the talk of the water-courses
everywhere in the hollows!

Nobody started it, nobody is going
to stop it. It will talk as long as it
wants, this rain. As long as it talks I
am going to listen.

—*Thomas Merton*

*Feel the soft wet rain. See the trees bow
and sway. Smell the forest fragrance
which rain releases. And listen, listen to
the rain "talk" as long as it wants.*

What does rain say about God's heart?

AND GOD SAID TO NOAH,
"THIS IS THE SIGN OF THE COVENANT I AM MAKING BETWEEN
ME AND YOU AND EVERY LIVING CREATURE WITH YOU,
A COVENANT FOR ALL GENERATIONS TO COME:
I HAVE SET MY RAINBOW IN THE CLOUDS."

GEN. 9:12-13 (NIV)

A rainbow is the result of storm and sun, the union of heaven and earth.
If you want to see rainbows, you have to endure the rain.

Consider when God's light has produced great beauty, even during stormy times in your life.

As the rain and the snow come
down from heaven,
and do not return to it without
watering the earth
and making it bud and flourish,
so that it yields seed for the
sower and bread for the eater,
so is my word that goes out from
my mouth:
It will not return to me empty,
but will accomplish what I desire
and achieve the purpose for
which I sent it.

Is. 55:10-11 (NIV)

Rainbows do not come cheap –
they are born out of the storm…
they come to those who weep.

— *Jan Sutch Pickard*

E arth's crammed with heaven,
    And every common bush afire
        with God;
But only he who sees,
    takes off his shoes,
The rest sit round it and
    pluck blackberries...

—*Elizabeth Barrett Browning*

Moses was going about his daily
chores, tending his flocks in the
desert when...

THE LORD APPEARED TO HIM IN
FLAMES OF FIRE FROM WITHIN A
BUSH. MOSES SAW THAT THOUGH
THE BUSH WAS ON FIRE IT DID NOT
BURN UP. SO MOSES THOUGHT,
"I WILL GO OVER AND SEE THIS
STRANGE SIGHT - WHY THE BUSH
DOES NOT BURN UP." WHEN THE
LORD SAW THAT HE HAD GONE OVER
TO LOOK, GOD CALLED TO HIM
FROM WITHIN THE BUSH, "MOSES!
MOSES!" AND MOSES SAID, "HERE
I AM."

EXODUS 3:2-4 (NIV)

The real miracle was that Moses
stopped and turned, and *then* God
called to him.

How can you pay more attention to the holy revealed on earth?

Stop and Listen
*to how God may be calling you,
even now, in this place.*

With few natural enemies, many redwoods survive for centuries. They can survive the worst of storms, and even when all upper growth is destroyed by wind or fire, these tenacious trees clone themselves. New growth sprouts almost immediately from burls forming a ring around the base of the tree trunk. Those receiving the most rain and light sprout and the saplings use the parent tree's roots for nourishment and stability. Redwoods are usually found in "family circles," clusters which support each other and ensure the survival of each tree.

AND LET US CONSIDER HOW WE MAY SPUR ONE ANOTHER ON TOWARD LOVE AND GOOD DEEDS. LET US NOT GIVE UP MEETING TOGETHER, AS SOME ARE IN THE HABIT OF DOING, BUT LET US ENCOURAGE ONE ANOTHER – AND ALL THE MORE AS YOU SEE THE DAY APPROACHING.

HEB.10:24, 25 (NIV)

Do you have a circle of friends or family who rely on you and to whom you look for support?

How can you deepen and strengthen your roots to endure trials with your community?

Would you describe your life as a canal, pouring forth to others?

Or is your life a reservoir, giving from God's fullness?

How is God inviting you to be "filled" this day?

The (one) who is wise, therefore, will see his life as more like a reservoir than a canal. The canal simultaneously pours out what it receives; the reservoir retains the water till it is filled, then discharges the overflow without loss to itself. He knows that a curse is on the (one) who allows his own property to degenerate. And if you think my opinion worthless, then listen to the one who is wiser than I: "The fool," said Solomon, "comes out with all his feelings at once, but the wise (person) subdues and restrains them."

Today there are many in the Church who act like canals, the reservoirs are far too rare. So urgent is the charity of those through whom the streams of heavenly doctrine flow to us, that they want to pour it forth before they have been filled; they are more ready to speak than to listen, impatient to teach what they have not grasped and full of presumption to govern others while they know not how to govern themselves.

— *Bernard of Clairvaux*

We learn over time and experience how to bring the reality of resting in God into the confusion and busyness and daily life. We learn to work resting.

We learn to live on two levels at once. On the one level we carry on the ordinary tasks of our day. But on a deeper level we live out of inward promptings and whispered words of wisdom. We learn to walk in the light wherever we may be, whomever we may be with, and whatever we may be doing.

To be sure we are working, but we are working resting. There is a rest for the people of God, says the writer of Hebrews, and we are entering into this divine rest.

—Richard J. Foster and
Gayle D. Beebe

When you watch this river flow, you cannot see its undercurrent moving deep below, often in a direction different than water on the surface. Yet, that strong, steady flow moves the river toward its destination.

In a similar way, God's deep, abiding love moves and carries you. It gives you an invisible source of rest beneath the work. People may notice your activity, but the undercurrent of rest gives your work power and vitality.

Rest provides freedom from care and worry and sin, a security that is rare in our culture.

How do you experience this essential life-giving rest from God? How can you be more aware of this underlying influence in your life?

Two roads diverged in a yellow wood,
And sorry I could not travel both
And be one traveler, long I stood
And looked down one as far as I could
To where it bent in the undergrowth;

Then took the other, as just as fair,
And having perhaps the better claim,
Because it was grassy and wanted wear;
Though as for that the passing there
Had worn them really about the same,

And both that morning equally lay
In leaves no step had trodden black.
Oh, I kept the first for another day!
Yet knowing how way leads on to way,
I doubted if I should ever come back.

I shall be telling this with a sigh
Somewhere ages and ages hence:
Two roads diverged in a wood, and I –
I took the one less traveled by,
And that has made all the difference.

—*Robert Frost*

*Consider choices
you have made—
roads followed and
roads abandoned.*

*How do your
experiences
influence your
decisions now?*

Many years ago there lived in a small village, in a country far away, a very wise and respected sage. He was often asked by visitors how he had become so wise. "Where did you study? Who was your teacher?" they asked. On one occasion the old man replied, "To this day, I have many teachers, and my studies continue in the woods and mountains that surround my village." Then his face became radiant and content. Gazing up at the forested slopes of the mountains he softly added, "I have learned many valuable lessons there."

"The rocks were among my first teachers. From them I have learned how to sit and be still. Once I did this, I began to notice everything around me in a new way. An oak tree taught me the difference one life can make: I saw how this oak and its brethren warmed the cold winter and made the summer's heat more pleasant; how the forest animals came to the tree for shelter, food, and comfort. Since then I have tried to live for others."

—*Author Unknown*

God uses nature to teach us truths about God and about ourselves. Sit and be still in this place with a teachable heart.

W ho among us is not captured by the mystery of seeds suddenly sprouting from the earth? It is fascinating to plant a garden and watch the fledgling green sprouts, ripe with the promise of new birth – and flowers or yummy vegetables in the months ahead!

God invites us to pay attention to the mystery that is within us. Thomas Merton says that each moment and event plants spiritual seeds in our souls. But, he cautions, most seeds die because the soil of our inner life is not ready to receive them. "Such seeds as these cannot spring up anywhere except in the good soil of freedom, spontaneity and love."

Jesus repeatedly used images from nature to teach his disciples, inviting them to "consider the birds of the air," and "the lilies of the field." (Matt. 6:26, 28)

Open your eyes! Change the way you perceive the world and be receptive to God's presence. Jesus' view challenges our culture as much as it did his early followers. In a world often perceived as impersonal and routine, Jesus calls us to be aware of the dynamic, ever-changing life around us.

What is being "birthed" in you? Is your inner soil prepared for the growth God offers to you?

Sit beneath a Sequoia
or other large tree
and meditate on
the images from this
prayer.

Take whatever time
you need to become
"grounded" and to
rediscover your roots.

SEQUOIA PRAYER

When I feel tiny, weak, and trembling
Or pulled this way and that by swirls of change,
Too insignificant to be of service,
Too "uprooted" to hold my ground,
I pray my Sequoia Prayer.

Sitting quietly, breathing normally,
becoming centered in the present moment –
in this holy instant –
My mind's eye gradually forms an image of a giant Sequoia.
My Sequoia prayer takes form in my heart and soul
As the image forms and fleshes out to fill my being.

Centuries-old roots so wide and deep they have become part of the earth,
Supporting enormous, gnarled trunk that soars into the sky,
Eternity wrinkles carved into its surface, holding character markings for the ages,
Thick, porous bark skin covering the body, letting the trunk breathe,
protecting it from the fires that must come to support its growth,
Green leaves gushing out the top, reaching up to the heavens,
Nurturing birds and other beings, offering up limbs as if in prayer.

Awareness of God fills my soul.
Sequoia image fills my being.

Spreading
Down into the earth,
Deep into the soul,
Strong into the body.

Breathing calmly, sitting quietly, praying trustingly, becoming
Grounded in humanity,
Rooted in God,
Striving ever upward.
My Sequoia prayer fills my cells, my lungs, my heart, my brain, my soul, my being
With love, grace, light.
With joy, hope.

With the strength of God I need to go on! Thank you, God!
Amen.

— *Dr. Monteen Lucas*

A common problem, related to why we may seek to escape silence, is the discovery that it evokes nameless misgivings, guilt feelings, strange, disquieting anxiety. Anything is better than this mess, and so we flick on the radio or pick up the phone and talk to a friend. If we can pass through these initial fears and remain silent, we may experience a gradual waning of inner chaos. Silence becomes like a creative space in which we regain perspective on the whole.

—*Susan Annette Muto*

We spend the bulk of our days talking – or anticipating what we will say next. Our chattering minds keep us from really listening to those around us or experiencing the lessons of nature before us. Instead of a conversation, our prayer life often consists of too much talking and too little listening.

Don't become discouraged if the quiet of this day awakens you to the noise within. This is common. The longer you fight this chaos, the longer you won't be truly still. Wait as long as it takes. Be still. Don't give up. Inner peace is worth the wait.

You cannot perceive beauty but with a serene mind.
—*Henry David Thoreau*

GOD SAID TO THE ISRAELITES:
IN REPENTANCE AND REST IS YOUR SALVATION,
IN QUIETNESS AND TRUST IS YOUR STRENGTH,
BUT YOU WOULD HAVE NONE OF IT.

Is. 30:15 (NIV)

MY HEART IS NOT PROUD, O LORD, MY EYES ARE NOT HAUGHTY;
I DO NOT CONCERN MYSELF WITH GREAT MATTERS
OR THINGS TOO WONDERFUL FOR ME.
BUT I HAVE STILLED AND QUIETED MY SOUL;
LIKE A WEANED CHILD WITH ITS MOTHER,
LIKE A WEANED CHILD IS MY SOUL WITHIN ME.

Ps. 131:1-2 (NIV)

Those who serve others sometimes feel selfish and guilty if they seek solitude and silence. Paradoxically, the busier and more restless we become, the more we need to seek time alone to refresh and renew us. See how all of nature grows in silence. The more God meets us in silent prayer, the more we have to give to others.

We need times of solitude and silence to buttress the demands of each day. As you seek assurance from the One who knows all secrets, the quietness of this spot welcomes your deepest prayers and silent longings.

How are you being weaned from loving God for your own needs and desires to loving and trusting God for God's own sake?

BE STILL AND KNOW THAT I AM GOD.
Ps. 46:10 (NIV)

What burdens
are you carrying
today?

Take time to
release them into
God's care, that
you may be fully
present in this place
on this day.

S implicity is one of the most valuable lessons we can learn from nature. We experience a certain freedom by traveling lightly on the path, unencumbered by unnecessary food, clothing, or gadgets. We need to adopt an inner simplicity by also leaving behind confused thoughts and agendas.

Each day we carry an enormous load of emotional and material baggage. The weight prevents us from straightening up to see and experience the beauty of each moment. Worries and anxieties give us spiritual cataracts.

Simplify, simplify, simplify.
—*Henry David Thoreau*

GIVE ALL YOUR WORRIES AND CARES TO GOD, FOR HE CARES ABOUT YOU.

I PETER 5:7 (NLT)

Don't merely push all your concerns away while you're here in these woods. Instead, pay attention to what forest creatures can teach you about life's complexities.

The spider simply weaves its web
without vanity or striving.
Finishing in due course,
then it waits.

Each forest creature does the same,
follows its way without resistance or denial,
being simply what it is,
living its unexamined life.

What can I learn from those "thoughtless"
creatures about reflection and self-awareness?
They are who they are
without concern or abstraction.

The forest calls me to discover who I am,
to cultivate an inner and outer awareness,
to be keenly aware of the world around me,
and the spirit within me.

You who gave the spider such a single heart,
attune my soul to live deliberately, carefully, naturally,
to find a balance between striving and waiting,
between resistance and resignation.

Teach me to do one thing at a time.

— *Robert M. Hamma*

How are you invited to "do one thing at a time," to simplify your life?

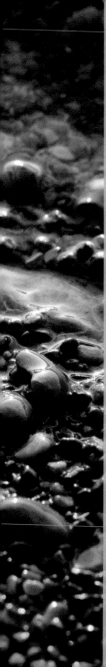

Does God really mean for us to find joy in our trials? Certainly patience and perseverance—but joy? How can we find genuine joy when we are confused, depressed, sick, worried about finances, or grieving a death or broken relationship?

Polished pebbles cover many riverbeds. Years of tossing and tumbling in swift water wears them to silky smoothness. Just as God uses the turbulent waters to smooth off the rough edges of the rocks, God uses our troubles to smooth off the rough edges of our character, refining our souls to be "mature and complete." It is a slow process, and results are difficult to see in the chaos and darkness. But we can trust that God is indeed at work.

Choose a smooth pebble from the water and carry it in your pocket as a reminder of how God is refining you, especially when you are suffering.

BE CAREFUL,
AND WATCH
YOURSELVES
CLOSELY SO THAT
YOU DO NOT
FORGET THE
THINGS YOUR EYES
HAVE SEEN, OR LET
THEM SLIP FROM
YOUR HEART AS
LONG AS YOU LIVE.
TEACH THEM TO
YOUR CHILDREN
AND TO THEIR
CHILDREN AFTER
THEM.

DEUT. 4:9 (NIV)

When the Israelites crossed the Jordan River, the very first thing God told them to do was to build a memorial from stones in the riverbed, instructing that when their children asked in the future, "WHAT DO THESE STONES MEAN?" TELL THEM THAT THE FLOW OF THE JORDAN WAS CUT OFF BEFORE THE ARK OF THE COVENANT OF THE LORD... THESE STONES ARE TO BE A MEMORIAL TO THE PEOPLE OF ISRAEL FOREVER.

JSH. 4:6-7 (NIV)

The most basic command of Scripture is to remember. God didn't want remembering His activity and blessing to be difficult for us and made it as simple as possible—even using piles of rocks.

When you look back and remember times when God healed, rescued, or sustained you, your faith grows. When David faced King Saul, he didn't just decide to 'have more faith.' David remembered what God had already done in his life: "THE LORD WHO DELIVERED ME FROM THE PAW OF THE LION AND THE PAW OF THE BEAR WILL DELIVER ME FROM THE HAND OF THIS PHILISTINE."

I SAM. 17:37 (NIV)

Alan Wright says, "Yesterday's God Moments are stones in the sling of Faith for tomorrow's giants. Our faith is built upon the actual, historical activity of God."

Where are your stones? Where is your memorial to the good gifts God has given you? Take time today to erect a pile of rocks, remembering the times God has met your needs.

Using stones, cross a creek one step at a time. If it is a wide or deep stream, you
may need others to help you find or build a way across. Name the people, circumstances,
and experiences in your life that are stumbling blocks.
What needs to happen for them to transform into "stepping stones"?

Unsure, when what was bright
turns dark and life, it seems, has
lost its way, we question what we
once believed and fear that doubt has
come to stay.

We sense the worm that gnaws within
has withered willpower, weakened bones,
and wonder whether all that's left
is stumbling blocks or stepping stones.

Where minds and bodies reel with pain
which nervous smiles can never mask,

and hope is forced to face despair
and all the things it dared not ask;
aware of weakness, guilt or shame,
the will gives out, the spirit groans,
and clutching at each straw we find
more stumbling blocks
than stepping stones.

Where family life has lost its bliss
and silences endorse mistrust,
or anger boils and tempers flare
as love comes under threat from lust;

where people cannot take the strain
of worklessness and endless loans
what pattern will the future weave –
just stumbling blocks? no stepping stones?

Where hearts that once held love are
bare and faith, in shreds, compounds the
mess; where hymns and prayers no longer
speak and former friends no longer bless;
and when the church where some
belonged no more their loyalty enthrones,
the plea is made, "If you are there,

turn stumbling blocks to stepping stones."

Ah God, You with the Maker's eye,
can tell if all that's feared is real,
and see if life is more than what
we suffer, dread, despise and feel.
If some by faith no longer stand
nor hear the truth Your voice intones,
stretch out Your hand to help Your
folk from stumbling blocks to stepping
stones.

—*John Bell and Graham Maule*

O most High, almighty, good Lord God,
to you belong praise, glory, honor, and all blessing!

Praised by my Lord God with all creatures;
and especially our Brother the Sun,
which brings us the day and the light;
fair is he, and shining with a very great splendor:
O Lord, he signifies you to us!

Praised be my Lord for our Sister the Moon,
and for the stars,
which God has set clear and lovely in heaven.

Praised be my Lord for our Brother the Wind,
and for air and cloud, calms and all weather,
by which you uphold in life all creatures.

Praised be my Lord for our Sister Water,
which is very serviceable to us,
and humble, and precious, and clean.

Praised be my Lord for Brother Fire,
through which you give us light in the darkness;
and he is bright, and pleasant, and very mighty,
and strong.

Praised be my Lord for our Sister the Earth,
which sustains us and keeps us,
and yields diverse fruits, and flowers of many colors, and grass.

Praised be my Lord for all those who pardon
one another for God's love's sake,
and who endure weakness and tribulation;
blessed are they who peaceably shall endure,
for you, O most High, shall give them a crown!

Praised be my Lord for our Sister,
the death of the body, from which no one escapes,
Woe to him who died in mortal sin!

Blessed are they who are found walking
by your most holy will,
for the second death shall have no
power to do them harm.

Praise you, and bless you the Lord
and give thanks to God, and serve God with great humility.

— *St. Francis of Assisi*

Write your own verses of praise to God for creation.
What fills you with joy and thanksgiving?

*How have you
experienced God's
tender care?*

*Do you sense
God's invitation
to draw near to his
heart today?*

When I see sunbeams stretching through the clouds to touch the earth, I think of God's fingers extending tender mercies to us. As these verses express, God seeks us, offering to rescue us from danger, strengthen us in trials, and comfort us in need. God is personal and intimate, not aloof and remote.

HE REACHED DOWN FROM ON HIGH AND TOOK HOLD OF ME; HE DREW ME OUT OF DEEP WATERS.

Ps. 18:16 (NIV)

SO DO NOT FEAR, FOR I AM WITH YOU; DO NOT BE DISMAYED, FOR I AM YOUR GOD. I WILL STRENGTHEN YOU AND HELP YOU; I WILL UPHOLD YOU WITH MY RIGHTEOUS RIGHT HAND.

Is. 41:10 (NIV)

HE TENDS HIS FLOCK LIKE A SHEPHERD; HE GATHERS THE LAMBS IN HIS ARMS AND CARRIES THEM CLOSE TO HIS HEART; HE GENTLY LEADS THOSE THAT HAVE YOUNG.

Is. 40:11 (NIV)

P raise to You, Adonai our God,
from whom the evening flows.
Your wisdom sets the way on
which time and season glide;
Your breath guides the sail of the stars.
Creator of the tide of time and light,
You guide the current of day into night.
As heaven spans to infinity,
You set its course for eternity.
Praise to You, Adonai our God,
from whom the evening flows.
This is an hour of change.
Within it we stand uncertain on the
border of light.
Shall we draw back or cross over?
Where shall our hearts turn?
Shall we draw back, my brother,
my sister, or cross over?
This is the hour of change, and within it,
we stand quietly on the border of light.
What lies before us?
Shall we draw back, my brother,
my sister, or cross over?

HEBREW SHABBAT EVENING PRAYER

*Too often people watch the sun drop
below the horizon and then depart, but
that's when the real show begins! If we
continue to "stand quietly on the border
of light," the sky explodes with a host of
colors. If you are fortunate to be viewing
such a sunset now, wait patiently to see
the gift that will unfold.*

As you gaze in this "hour of change," what needs to change in your own life. Will you "draw back," or cross over?"

A MAN WAS THERE NAMED
ZACCHAEUS; HE WAS A CHIEF
TAX COLLECTOR AND WAS RICH.
HE WAS TRYING TO SEE WHO JESUS WAS,
BUT ON ACCOUNT OF THE CROWD HE
COULD NOT, BECAUSE HE WAS SHORT
IN STATURE. SO HE RAN AHEAD AND
CLIMBED A SYCAMORE TREE TO SEE
HIM, BECAUSE HE WAS GOING TO PASS
THAT WAY. WHEN JESUS CAME TO THE
PLACE, HE LOOKED UP AND SAID TO
HIM, "ZACCHAEUS, HURRY AND COME
DOWN; FOR I MUST STAY AT YOUR HOUSE
TODAY." SO HE HURRIED DOWN AND WAS
HAPPY TO WELCOME HIM.

LUKE 19:1-6 (NRSV)

The sycamore tree gave Zacchaeus
a new perspective on his life and
the person of Jesus. He was rich in
earthly possessions, but lonely and
unfulfilled. He was also full of curiosity
and willing to take a risk, even doing
something oddly childish, to find more
meaning in his life. His encounter with
Jesus transformed his life.

*How might you
do some curiosity-
climbing?*

*How might you
open your heart
and mind to a
new perspective on
yourself and your
God?*

This is my Father's world, And to my listening ears
All nature sings, and round me rings
The music of the spheres.
This is my Father's world: I rest me in the thought
Of rocks and trees, of skies and seas - His hand the wonders wrought.

This is my Father's world, the birds their carols raise,
The morning light, the lily white,
Declare their Maker's praise.
This is my Father's world: He shines in all that's fair;
In the rustling grass I hear Him pass, He speaks to me everywhere.

This is my Father's world, O let me ne'er forget
that though the wrong seems oft so strong,
God is the Ruler yet.
This is my Father's world: Why should my heart be sad?
The Lord is King: let the heavens ring!
God reigns: let earth be glad!

—*Malthie D. Babcock*

*Every purely natural object is a
conductor of divinity.*—*John Muir*

*Holy Earth Mother, the trees and all
nature are witnesses of your thoughts and
deeds.*—*Winnebago Indian Prayer*

*If the doors of perception were cleansed,
everything would be seen as it is, infinite.*
—*William Blake*

*As you walk,
give thanks for
the way nature
manifests God in
this place.*

A tree gives glory to God by being a tree. For in being what God means it to be it is obeying Him. It 'consents,' so to speak, to His creative love. It is expressing an idea which is in God and which is not distinct from the essence of God, and therefore a tree imitates God by being a tree. The more a tree is like itself, the more it is like Him. If it tried to be something else which it was never intended to be, it would be less like God and therefore it would give Him less glory.

—*Thomas Merton*

How is God calling you to be your authentic self?
What do you need to lay down or pick up?
Give thanks to God for the way you are uniquely created.

An old Chinese folktale describes a student asking his teacher what to do with a seemingly useless tree. Its branches were too knotted and twisted to build anything serviceable.

The wise teacher responds that the tree is only useless because the student is trying to make it something it is not. Though it will never become a piece of furniture or the straight beam of a rooftop, it does provide shelter for wildlife and shade for weary travelers. He suggests that the student appreciate the gnarled tree for its unique design and resist trying to use it in unsuitable ways.

Who have you dismissed as "not useful"?

What would be different if you viewed this person with God's eyes?

A FARMER WENT OUT TO SOW HIS SEED...SOME FELL ON ROCKY PLACES, WHERE IT DID NOT HAVE MUCH SOIL. IT SPRANG UP QUICKLY, BECAUSE THE SOIL WAS SHALLOW. BUT WHEN THE SUN CAME UP, THE PLANTS WERE SCORCHED, AND THEY WITHERED BECAUSE THEY HAD NO ROOT.

THE ONE WHO RECEIVED THE SEED THAT FELL ON ROCKY PLACES IS THE MAN WHO HEARS THE WORD AND AT ONCE RECEIVES IT WITH JOY. BUT SINCE HE HAS NO ROOT, HE LASTS ONLY A SHORT TIME. WHEN TROUBLE OR PERSECUTION COMES BECAUSE OF THE WORD, HE QUICKLY FALLS AWAY.

MATT. 13: 3-6, 20-21 (NIV)

What needs to happen for your roots to grow deep in fertile soil?

MAKE EVERY EFFORT TO LIVE IN PEACE WITH ALL MEN AND TO BE HOLY; WITHOUT HOLINESS NO ONE WILL SEE THE LORD. SEE TO IT THAT NO ONE MISSES THE GRACE OF GOD AND THAT NO BITTER ROOT GROWS UP TO CAUSE TROUBLE AND DEFILE MANY.

HEB. 12:14-15 (NIV)

Ask God to reveal any "root of bitterness" that may be growing within you.

Identify it and ask God what needs to happen to weed it out.

HAPPY ARE THOSE WHO
DO NOT FOLLOW THE ADVICE
OF THE WICKED OR TAKE THE
PATH THAT SINNERS TREAD, OR SIT IN
THE SEAT OF SCOFFERS; BUT THEIR DE-
LIGHT IS IN THE LAW OF THE LORD, AND
ON HIS LAW THEY MEDITATE DAY AND
NIGHT. THEY ARE LIKE TREES PLANTED
BY STREAMS OF WATER, WHICH YIELD
THEIR FRUIT IN ITS SEASON, AND
THEIR LEAVES DO NOT WITHER.
IN ALL THAT THEY DO,
THEY PROSPER.

PS. 1:1-3 (NRSV)

Sit or *lean* against "your" tree.
Feel the roots of your soul sinking
down into the humus and nourishing
strength of God's Spirit. Reach
up toward the sky, allowing the
refreshing sun and rain of God's
love to embrace you.

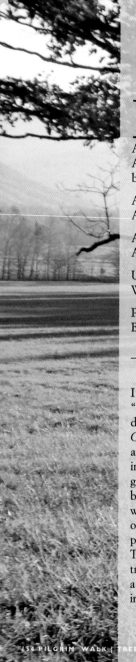

I think that I shall never see
A poem lovely as a tree.

A tree whose hungry mouth is prest
Against the earth's sweet flowing
breast;

A tree that looks at God all day,
And lifts her leafy arms to pray;

A tree that may in Summer wear
A nest of robins in her hair;

Upon whose bosom snow has lain;
Who intimately lives with rain.

Poems are made by fools like me,
But only God can make a tree.

—*Joyce Kilmer*

I discovered a helpful game called
"Meet a Tree" in Joseph Cornell's
delightful book *Sharing Nature with
Children.* Take a friend to a forest,
and then blindfold her. Using an
indirect route, lead her to a tree and
give her time to feel the tree's size,
bark, branches, and leaves, along
with its lichens or any plants growing
on it. Next, return to your starting
point and remove the blindfold.
Then let your friend try to choose the
tree from all the others. "What was
a forest becomes a collection of very
individual trees."

TREES | PILGRIM WALK 155

Some flowers are cultivated to be picked and arranged in gorgeous bouquets, but many wildflowers need to be protected and enjoyed where they are naturally growing.

One such wildflower is the delicate trillium, which blooms in early spring in shady forests. When a careless person picks the flower and its stem with leaves attached, he strips the stalk of its sustenance for the following season. Without its petals and leaves, the flower cannot produce food, and years may pass before it can recover and bloom again.

Friendships can be just as delicate. To grow and blossom, they require careful tending. When we are careless or unkind to friends, we must earn back their trust and respect, or they disappear altogether.

Is there a friendship you have damaged or failed to cultivate?

What needs to happen for that to be restored?

Do you need to ask forgiveness?

Do you need to forgive a friend who hurt you in order to grow again?

Have you experienced
God's pruning of
people, activities, or
possessions in your
life which felt painful
at the time but has
produced abundant
fruit?

How can you abide
in God's goodness
today?

Abide in me...Make your home in me...
Remain in me....Live in me...

I AM THE TRUE VINE, AND MY FATHER IS THE VINEGROWER. HE REMOVES EVERY BRANCH IN ME THAT BEARS NO FRUIT. EVERY BRANCH THAT BEARS FRUIT HE PRUNES TO MAKE IT BEAR MORE FRUIT...

ABIDE IN ME AS I ABIDE IN YOU. JUST AS THE BRANCH CANNOT BEAR FRUIT BY ITSELF UNLESS IT ABIDES IN THE VINE, NEITHER CAN YOU UNLESS YOU ABIDE IN ME. I AM THE VINE, YOU ARE THE BRANCHES. THOSE WHO ABIDE IN ME AND I IN THEM BEAR MUCH FRUIT, BECAUSE APART FROM ME YOU CAN DO NOTHING.

JOHN 15: 1-2, 4-5 (NRSV)

Just as the life-giving sap runs from the the vine to the branches, God's unseen power nourishes and sustains us if we stay connected. We respond to the loving care of the Gardener not by *doing* anything, but simply by responding to the necessary discipline and pruning we need to live fruitful lives.

Just as a wise parent disciplines a child, a careful vinegrower prunes the plant to produce abundant fruit. Vines can become so dense that sun cannot penetrate. Though the leaves look healthy, the branches fail to fulfill their intended purpose—to produce grapes. In the same way, misplaced priorities in our lives can hinder us from staying connected and living an abundant life. God is faithful to cut away distractions and restore true purpose.

A pilgrim looked at the reflection of a mountain in still water. It was the reflection that first caught his attention. But presently he raised his eyes to the mountain. "Reflect Me," said his Father to him, "then others will look at you. Then they will look up, and see me. And the stiller the water the more perfect the reflection."

—*Amy Carmichael*

AND WE, WHO WITH UNVEILED FACES ALL
REFLECT THE LORD'S GLORY, ARE BEING
TRANSFORMED INTO HIS LIKENESS WITH
EVER-INCREASING GLORY, WHICH COMES
FROM THE LORD, WHO IS THE SPIRIT.

II COR. 3:18 (NIV)

Choose two small stones.
Throw one into the water as a symbol of
something in your life that you would like to
leave behind in this place. Take the other back
with you as a sign of a new commitment in
your heart.

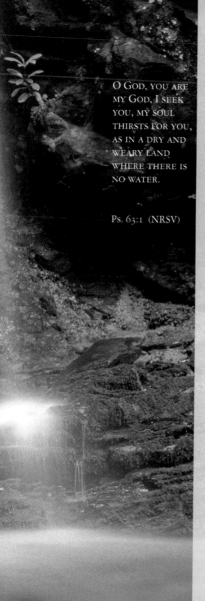

O God, you are my God, I seek you, my soul thirsts for you, as in a dry and weary land where there is no water.

Ps. 63:1 (NRSV)

Thirst is a metaphor for spiritual needs and a constant theme in the Bible:

Ho, everyone who thirsts come
    to the waters;
and you that have no money,
come,
    buy, and eat!
Why do you spend your money...
and labor for that which
    does not satisfy?
Listen carefully to me, and
    eat what is good,
and delight yourselves in rich
food.
Come to me; listen, so that
    you may live.

Is. 55:1-3 (NRSV)

As the deer longs for flowing
streams,
so my soul longs for you, O God.
My soul thirsts for God, for the
    living God.
When shall I come and behold
the face of God?

Ps. 42:1-2 (NRSV)

What are you thirsting for in your life?

Observe the waterfall's unique gifts. Is it a gentle trickle or a thundering crash? Do you see rising mist or a shimmering rainbow? Feel the mist on your skin or wade into the pools below.

Out of the mists and the clouds with a leap
    and a shuddering cry
The waterfall, red with the blood of the earth,
crashes to death with a sigh,
Down past the shivering trees to the rocks
    where its waters die
To arise in a vapor of ghostly forms
    seeking again the sky.
They weave from the threads of the sun
    a rainbow of tremulous light
While the sound of their dying sighs is
    the voice of a storm in its might.
The mountains in beauty dressed
    stand awed by that magical sight
Of the wedding of heaven and earth
    in a waterfall's headlong flight.

— *Zhang Jiuling*

How is the waterfall a metaphor for heaven and earth meeting?

To watch water gently springing from the earth is to witness creation in an act of unconditional generosity. This holy well can be a symbol of the source of life within, from which spring hopes and dreams. Here, we can tend to our inner holy well which often becomes clogged and concealed by anxieties and busyness.

Healing God, come to our
hidden corners.
Remove the stone and grit
that we cling to,
that prevent the water of life
flowing free.

—*Rita Minehan*

*Sit by the well
and rest awhile.
Drink and
nourish yourself.*

We did not think of the great open plains, the beautiful rolling hills and winding streams of tangled growth as "wild." Only to the white man was nature "wilderness" and only to him was the land "infested" with "wild" animals and "savage" people. To us it was tame. Earth was bountiful and we were surrounded with the blessings of the Great Mystery...

When the very animals of the forest began fleeing from his approach then it was that the "wild west" began.

—*Chief Luther Standing Bear*

What value do you see in wilderness places?
How willing are you to sacrifice in order to protect and
preserve the wilderness?

Like winds and sunsets, wild things were taken for granted until progress began to do away with them. Now we face the question whether a still higher "standard of living" is worth its cost in things natural, wild and free. For us of the minority, the opportunity to see geese is more important than television, and the chance to find a pasque-flower is a right as inalienable as free speech.

—*Aldo Leopold*

*If God gives such attention to wildflowers and birds,
most of which are never even seen, don't you think he'll attend
to you, take pride in you, and give you his best?*

THERE IS FAR MORE TO YOUR LIFE THAN THE FOOD YOU PUT IN YOUR STOMACH, MORE TO YOUR OUTER APPEARANCE THAN THE CLOTHES YOU HANG ON YOUR BODY. LOOK AT THE BIRDS, FREE AND UNFETTERED, NOT TIED DOWN TO A JOB DESCRIPTION, CARELESS IN THE CARE OF GOD. AND YOU COUNT FAR MORE TO HIM THAN BIRDS.

HAS ANYONE BY FUSSING IN FRONT OF THE MIRROR EVER GOTTEN TALLER BY SO MUCH AS AN INCH? ALL THIS TIME AND MONEY WASTED ON FASHION - DO YOU THINK IT MAKES THAT MUCH DIFFERENCE? INSTEAD OF LOOKING AT THE FASHIONS, WALK OUT INTO THE FIELDS AND LOOK AT THE WILDFLOWERS. THEY NEVER PRIMP OR SHOP, BUT HAVE YOU EVER SEEN COLOR AND DESIGN QUITE LIKE IT? THE TEN BEST-DRESSED MEN AND WOMEN

IN THE COUNTRY LOOK SHABBY ALONGSIDE THEM. IF GOD GIVES SUCH ATTENTION TO THE APPEARANCE OF WILDFLOWERS - MOST OF WHICH ARE NEVER EVEN SEEN - DON'T YOU THINK HE'LL ATTEND TO YOU, TAKE PRIDE IN YOU, DO HIS BEST FOR YOU? WHAT I'M TRYING TO DO HERE IS TO GET YOU TO RELAX, TO NOT BE SO PREOCCUPIED WITH GETTING, SO THAT YOU CAN RESPOND TO GOD'S GIVING...DON'T WORRY ABOUT MISSING OUT. YOU'LL FIND ALL YOUR EVERYDAY HUMAN CONCERNS WILL BE MET. GIVE YOUR ENTIRE ATTENTION TO WHAT GOD IS DOING RIGHT NOW, AND DON'T GET WORKED UP ABOUT WHAT MAY OR MAY NOT HAPPEN TOMORROW. GOD WILL HELP YOU DEAL WITH WHATEVER HARD THINGS COME UP WHEN THE TIME COMES.

MATTHEW 6: 25-34 (THE MESSAGE)

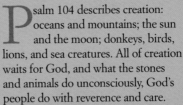

THESE ALL LOOK
TO YOU TO GIVE
THEM THEIR FOOD
IN DUE SEASON;
WHEN YOU GIVE
IT TO THEM, THEY
GATHER IT UP;
WHEN YOU OPEN
YOUR HAND, THEY
ARE FILLED WITH
GOOD THINGS.
Ps. 104:27-28
(NRSV)

MY SOUL,
WAIT ONLY
UPON GOD!

Ps. 62:5 (AMP)

Psalm 104 describes creation: oceans and mountains; the sun and the moon; donkeys, birds, lions, and sea creatures. All of creation waits for God, and what the stones and animals do unconsciously, God's people do with reverence and care.

The animals do not worry about the future, about their health, about their families, or about food and shelter. They bask in the beauty of their world, trusting by instinct that their needs will be met.

Nature offers a vivid reminder of our relationship to God. Just as we have no power to create life out of nothing, we have no power to sustain it. Yet, God does not abandon creation. We can depend on God. When we wait on God, we find rest, peace, purpose, joy, strength, and provision for all our needs.

The very purpose of God's creation is to show the riches of His goodness and power. Andrew Murray says that just as God is "unceasingly the supplier of every want in the creature, so the very place and nature of the creature is...to wait upon God and receive from Him what He alone can give, what He delights to give...We may rest assured that He who made us for Himself...will never disappoint us."

How is God calling you to wait today?
What worries do you need to place in God's hands?

Jesus said, NO ONE CAN ENTER
THE KINGDOM OF GOD WITHOUT
BEING BORN OF WATER AND THE
SPIRIT. A PERSON IS BORN PHYSICALLY
OF HUMAN PARENTS, BUT IS BORN
SPIRITUALLY OF THE SPIRIT. DO NOT BE
SURPRISED BECAUSE I TELL YOU THAT
YOU MUST ALL BE BORN AGAIN. THE
WIND BLOWS WHEREVER IT WISHES;
YOU HEAR THE SOUND IT MAKES, BUT
YOU DO NOT KNOW WHERE IT COMES
FROM OR WHERE IT IS GOING. IT IS
LIKE THAT WITH EVERYONE WHO IS
BORN OF THE SPIRIT.

JOHN 3:5-8 (GNT)

Rest in this place and be fully aware
of the wind.
See how it causes the leaves
and grasses to sway.
Hear its quiet stirring.
Feel its gentle caress on your skin.
Imagine God's Spirit blowing within
you, bringing you new life.

[GOD] MAKES WINDS HIS
MESSENGERS...

Ps. 104:4 (NIV)

What is the message you
hear in the wind?

END OF WALK

Hopefully, God has opened your heart and mind to new possibilities on your Pilgrim Walk and surprised you with new challenges and expressions of God's love and faithfulness.

Perhaps you are still pondering things you've heard today, or perhaps you heard a clear call to change. You now must decide whether to risk a new way of living, and as you discern God's invitation to a new way of being, remember that you are not alone. Other pilgrims join you on the road, sharing stories, tears, laughter, and a God who loves us all.

The Celts were always on the move, finally settling in Ireland and Scotland. Whether your pilgrimage requires an arduous journey over a lifetime or a day spent in the woods, it is an outward expression of an inner movement toward deeper faith and holiness. These prayers speak to all of us traveling the path to God.

Bless to us, O God
The moon that is above us,
The earth that is beneath us,
The friends who are around us,
Your image deep within us.
CELTIC PRAYER

May the road rise to meet you.
May the wind always be at your back.
May the sun shine warm upon your face.
May the rains fall softly upon your fields,
May God hold you in the hollow of his hand.
CELTIC BLESSING

INDEX

A

A Few More Verses: Leaves of Gold; 38-39
Abbott, Lyman; 12-13
Abide; 158-159
ACORN; 12-13
AIR; 86-87, 98-99
Alan Wright; 132-133
Aldo Leopold; 168-169
Alexander, Cecil F.; 14-15
Alfred Lord Tennyson; 48-49
All Things Bright and Beautiful; 14-15
Amy Carmichael; 160-161
Andrew Murray; 172-173
ANIMAL; 24-25, 16-17
Annie Elizabeth Cheney; 18-19
Anxieties; 126-127
Anxious; 18-19
Ask Me to Dance; 54-55
Ask; 34-35
Assisi, St. Francis of; 136-137
Augustine, St.; 36-37
Aware; 118-119, 174-175, 80-81, 88-89

B

Babcock, Maltbie D.; 144-145
Balance; 128-129
Barbara Kingsolver; 24-25
be still; 116-117, 122-123, 124-125
BEARS; 76-77
Beauty; 46-47, 60-61
Beebe, Gayle D.; 112-113

BEES; 76-77
Bell, John; 30-31, 134-135
Bernard of Clairvaux; 110-111
BIRD(S); 12-13, 14-15, 16-17, 18-19, 20-21, 22-23, 24-25, 38-39, 64-65, 76-77, 118-119, 120-121, 170-171, 172-173
BIRDSONG; 24-25
Blake, William; 144-145
BLOOM(S); 26-27, 38-39, 50-51
BLOSSOM; 26-27
Born; 30-31
Boundaries; 46-47
Bouquet; 52-53
Bragg, Sir William; 22-23
BRANCH(ES); 26-27, 154-155, 158-159
Breath Prayer; 64-65
Browning, Elizabeth Barrett; 106-107
Bruce Larson; 54-55
BUD(S); 26-27, 50-51, 104-105
BUDDING BRANCH; 26-27
Burroughs, John; 86-87
BUSH; 106-107
BUTTERFLY; 28-29

C

Canticle of the Sun; 136-137
CATERPILLAR; 28-29
Cecil F. Alexander; 14-15
Celtic Blessing; 176-177
Celtic Prayer; 6-7, 74-75, 176-

177
Cemetery; 30-31
Change the World; 96-97
Charles R. Swindoll; 54-55
Charmichael, Amy; 160-161
Cheney, Annie Elizabeth; 18-19
Chief Luther Standing Bear; 168-169
Chinese folktale; 148-149
Choices; 34-35, 114-115
Clairvaux, Bernard of; 110-111
CLOUD(S); 32-33, 76-77, 80-81, 136-137, 138-139,
COCOON; 28-29
Columbanus, Saint; 74-75
Commonplace; 38-39
Community/Communities; 58-59, 108-109
Compliments; 52-53
Concerning the Nature of Things; 22-23
Coolidge, Susan; 38-39
1 Cor. 12:12-27; 58-59
1 Cor. 3:5-9; 44-45
2 Cor. 4:18; 80-81
2 Cor. 3:18; 160-161
Cornell, Joseph; 154-155
Corrie ten Boom; 52-53
CREATION; 26-27, 74-75
CREATOR; 74-75
CROSSROAD(S); 34-35
CROWS; 36-37
Curiosity; 142-143

D
DAFFODILS; 50-51
Damien, Father; 16-17
DANDELION; 38-39
Darkness; 28-29, 30-31, 88-89
David James Duncan; 94-95
Davies, W.D.; 72-73
Day, Dorothy; 96-97
Dedication; 2-3
DEEP WATER; 112-113
DEER; 24-25
Deuteronomy 4:9; 132-133
Dewitt Jones; 22-23, 64-65

Dickinson, Emily; 78-79
DIRT; 84-85
Dorothy Day; 96-97
Douglas Wood; 92-93
Dr. Monteen Lucas; 120-121
DRY GRASS; 40-41
Duncan, David James; 94-95

E
EARTH; 82-83, 42-43, 138-139
Elijah; 78-79
Elizabeth Barrett Browning; 106-107
Emily Dickinson; 78-79
Encouragement; 92-93
End Of Walk; 176-177
Entangles/Entangled; 70-71
Eph. 1:18; 26-27
Eph. 3:20; 50-51
Eph.3:20; 12-13
Ex. 3:2-4; 106-107
Exhale; 64-65

F
Fall Inside; 94-95
Falls In; 94-95
Father Damien; 16-17
FIELD(S); 44-45, 46-47, 86-87, 118-119, 170-171
FIG TREE; 56-57
Filled; 110-111
FIRE; 46-47, 106-107
FISH; 16-17, 64-65
FLOOD; 46-47
FLOWER(S); 14-15, 38-39, 40-41, 48-49, 50-51, 52-53, 68-69, 74-75, 76-77, 98-99, 118-119, 136-137, 156-157, 168-169
FLY; 68-69
Focus; 80-81
FOREST(S); 70-71, 102-103
Foster, Richard J.; 112-113
Friendship(s); 156-157
FROG(S); 54-55
Frost, Robert; 114-115

FRUIT TREE; 56-57
FRUIT(S); 14-15, 56-57, 136-137, 152-153, 158-159

G

Gal. 5:22-23; 56-57
GARDEN; 74-75, 76-77, 118-119
Gayle D. Beebe; 112-113
Gaze; 90-91
GEESE; 58-59
Gen. 28:16; 88-89
Gen. 9:12-13; 104-105
Gerard Manley Hopkins; 62-63
Gnarled; 148-149
God All Around Me; 60-61
God's Grandeur; 62-63
God's Majesty; 64-65
Goodrun, Nancy; 70-71
Graham Maule; 134-135
Grandeur; 62-63
GRASS/GRASSES; 40-41, 74-75, 136-137, 174-175
Gratitude; 64-65, 98-99
GROUNDHOGS; 24-25
Grow(ing); 50-51, 92-93
Growth; 92-93, 108-109

H

Hamma, Robert M.; 128-129
Hanh, Thich Nhat; 82-83
Hassell, Paul; 11, 32-33
Hassell, Susanne V.; 10, 80-81
Heb. 10:24-25; 108-109
Heb. 12:1; 70-71
Heb. 12:14-15; 150-151
Hebrew Shabbat Evening Prayer; 88-89, 140-141
Henri Nouwen; 84-85
Henry David Thoreau; 122-123, 126-127
High Tide In Tucson; 24-25
HILLS; 66-67, 100-101
Hoezee, Scott; 20-21
HOLE; 94-95
Hopkins, Gerard Manley; 62-63
Hub; 84-85

Humility; 16-17
HUMMINGBIRD; 68-69

I

Inhale; 64-65
INSECTS; 70-71
Invitation; 6-7
Is. 30:15; 124-125
Is. 40:11; 138-139
Is. 40:6-8; 40-41
Is. 41:10; 138-139
Is. 41:17-20; 100-101
Is. 45:3; 28-29
Is. 55: 1-3; 162-163
Is. 55:10-11; 104-105
Is. 55:12-13; 100-101

J

James 1:2-4; 130-131
James Stalker; 46-47
Jan Sutch Pickard; 104-105
Jer. 6:16; 34-35
Jiuling, Zhang; 164-165
Job 12:7-10, 38:4-7; 16-17
John 15:1-2; 4-5; 158-159
John 3:5-8; 174-175
John 4:14; 166-167
John 4:35b-38; 44-45
John Bell; 30-31, 134-135
John Burroughs; 86-87
John Muir, 76-77, 144-145
Jones, Dewitt; 22-23, 64-65
Joseph Cornell; 154-155
Joseph Wood Krutch; 86-87
Joshua 4:6-7; 132-133
Joyce Kilmer; 154-155
Julian Of Norwich; 90-91

K

Kilmer, Joyce; 154-155
1 Kings 19:8-13; 78-79
Kingsolver, Barbara; 24-25
Kiss(ed); 54-55
Krutch, Joseph Wood; 86-87
KUDZU; 70-71

L

Larson, Bruce; 54-55
Leaves Of Gold; 12-13
LEAVES; 26-27, 56-57, 102-
103, 152-153, 154-155, 156-
157, 158-159, 174-175
Leisure; 72-73
Leopold, Aldo; 168-169
LICHEN(S); 74-75, 154-155
LIGHT; 26-27, 30-31, 88-89,
98-99, 104-105, 108-109, 112-
113, 136-137, 140-141
LILY/LILIES; 76-77, 118-119
Listen; 78-79, 102-103, 106-
107
Listening; 122-123
*Longing For God: Seven Paths Of
Christian Devotion*; 112-113
Longings; 124-125
Lucas, Dr. Monteen; 120-121
Luke 19:1-6; 142-143
Lyman Abbott; 12-13

M

Maltbie D. Babcock; 144-145
Mark 11:12-14; 56-57
Matt. 11:28-29; 34-35
Matt. 13:3-6;20-21; 150-151
Matt. 25:35-36; 96-97
Matt. 6:25-34; 170-171
Matt. 6:26,28; 118-119
Matt. 6:26; 18-19
Matt. 6:28-29; 76-77
Matt. 9:37-38; 44-45
Maule, Graham; 134-135
MEADOW; 76-77
Meet A Tree; 154-155
Merton, Thomas; 36-37, 102-
103, 118-119, 146-147
Minehan, Rita; 166-167
MIST; 80-81
MOON; 38-39, 66-67, 172-
173
Morris, Renni; 112-113
Mother Teresa; 36-37, 94-95
MOUNTAIN(S); 66-67, 78-
79, 80-81, 100-101, 116-117,
160-161, 164-165, 172-173
MUD; 82-83
Muir, John; 76-77, 144-145
Murray, Andrew; 172-173
MUSHROOM; 84-85
Muto, Susan Annette; 122-123
My First Summer In The Sierra;
76-77

N

Nancy Goodrun; 70-71
Native American Prayer; 42-43
NATURE; 86-87
Navajo Prayer; 60-61
Nearness Of God; 88-89
NEST; 20-21, 36-37
New Seeds Of Contemplation;
146-147
NIGHT; 88-89
Norwich, Julian Of; 90-91
Notice/Noticing; 72-73, 116-
117
Nouwen, Henri; 84-85
NUT(S); 72-73, 90-91

O

OAK TREE; 116-117
OCEANS; 172-173
Of Earth And Sky; 92-93
Overflow; 110-111
Overheard In An Orchard; 18-19

P

PATH; 34-35
Paul Hassell; 11, 32-33
Pay Attention; 42-43, 70-71,
106-107, 128-129,
PEBBLE; 96-97
1 Pet. 5:7; 126-127
1 Pet. 5:7; 18-19
Pickard, Jan Sutch; 104-105
PINE TREE; 92-93, 100-101
PIT; 94-95
PLANT(S); 16-17, 44-45,
70-71
POLISHED PEBBLES; 130-
131

POND; 96-97
Pray With Your Body; 60-61
Prayer Of Seven Directions; 60-61
Presence; 88-89
Prunes/Pruning; 158-159
Ps. 1:1-3; 152-153
Ps. 104:27-28; 172-173
Ps. 104:4; 174-175
Ps. 118:24; 64-65
Ps. 121; 66-67
Ps. 131:1-2; 124-125
Ps. 139:1-2; 88-89
Ps. 139:14; 38-39
Ps. 18:16; 138-139
Ps. 19:2-5; 72-73
Ps. 34:8-9; 68-69
Ps. 40:1-2; 82-83
Ps. 42:1-2; 162-163
Ps. 46:10; 124-125
Ps. 62:1; 172-173
Ps. 63:1; 162-163
Ps. 65; 80-81
Ps. 8; 64-65
Ps. 84:3; 20-21
Purpose; 46-47

R
Raids On The Unspeakable; 102-103
Rain And The Rhinoceros; 102-103
RAIN; 76-77, 98-99, 100-101, 102-103, 104-105, 108-109, 154-155
RAINBOW; 164-165
RAINBOW(S); 104-105
Reap; 44-45
RED BUSH; 106-107
REDWOODS; 108-109
Refining; 130-131
Reflection; 160-161
Remember Creation: God's World Of Wonder And Delight; 20-21
Renewing; 100-101
Renni Morris; 112-113
RESERVOIR; 110-111

Rest; 34-35, 112-113, 172-173, 174-175,
Resting; 112-113
Richard J. Foster; 112-113
Rita Minehan; 166-167
RIVER; 112-113
Ro. 12:10; 156-157
ROAD(S); 114-115
Robert Frost; 114-115
Robert M. Hamma; 128-129
Robert Runcie; 42-43
ROBIN; 18-19
ROCK(S); 50-51, 74-75, 78-79, 80-81, 82-83, 116-117, 132-133, 164-165
ROOT(S); 48-49, 56-57, 70-71, 92-93, 108-109, 120-121, 150-151
Runcie, Robert; 42-43

S
Safe; 66-67
Saint Augustine; 36-37
Saint Francis Of Assisi; 136-137
Saint Patrick's Breastplate Prayer; 60-61
1 Sam. 17:37; 132-133
SAND SPOKES; 84-85
Scott Hoezee; 20-21
SEED(S); 24-25, 28-29, 44-45, 104-105, 118-119, 150-151,
Seeing; 86-87
Sequoia Prayer; 120-121
Sermons On The Song Of Songs; 110-111
Seven Cardinal Virtues; 46-47
SHADE; 12-13
Sharing Nature With Children; 154-155
Sharing; 58-59
SHEEP; 76-77
Shelter; 12-13, 92-93
Silence; 122-123, 124-125
Silent; 122-123, 124-125
Simplicity; 126-127
Simplify; 126-127, 128-129
Sings; 38-39

Sir William Bragg; 22-23
SKY; 38-39
Slow Down; 72-73
SMOOTH STONES; 130-131
SNOW; 100-101, 104-105
Soar; 22-23
SOARING BIRD; 22-23
Soil; 62-63, 92-93, 118-119, 150-151
Solitude; 124-125
Song; 24-25
Songs Of The Universe; 48-49
Songs; 20-21
Sow; 44-45
SPARROW; 18-19
SPIDER; 128-129
SPRING; 166-167
SPRINGS; 100-101
SPROUTS; 118-119
SQUIRRELS; 72-73, 76-77
St. Columbanus; 74-75
Stalker, James; 46-47
Stand; 72-73, 78-79
Standing Bear, Chief Luther; 168-169
Standing; 132-133
Stare; 72-73
STARS; 38-39, 64-65
STEPPING STONES; 134-135
Still; 50-51, 122-123, 160-161
STONE(S); 132-133, 160-161, 166-167, 172-173
STORM(S); 32-33, 104-105, 108-109
STREAMS; 162-163, 168-169
Stumbling Blocks; 134-135
Suffering; 130-131
SUN; 32-33, 38-39, 66-67, 104-105, 136-137, 172-173
SUNBEAMS; 138-139
SUNLIGHT; 24-25, 32-33
SUNSET(S); 32-33, 140-141, 168-169
SUNSHINE; 76-77
Support; 108-109
Susan Annette Muto; 122-123

Susan Coolidge; 38-39
Susanne Hassell; 10, 80-81
Swindoll, Charles R.; 54-55
SYCAMORE TREE; 142-143

T

Ten Boom, Corrie; 52-53
Tennyson, Alfred Lord; 48-49
Teresa, Mother; 36-37, 94-95
The Gospel Of Nature; 86-87
The Miracle Of Mindfulness; 82-83
The Road Not Taken; 114-115
The Tale Of The Tardy Oxcart; 54-55
Thich Nhat Hanh; 82-83
Thirst; 162-163
Thirsting; 162-163
This Is My Father's World; 144-145
Thomas Merton; 36-37, 102-103, 118-119, 146-147
Thoreau, Henry David; 122-123, 126-127
Tips For The Journey; 8-9
TREE ROOTS; 150-151, 152-153
TREE(S); 24-25, 46-47, 50-51, 56-57, 68-69, 100-101, 102-103, 108-109, 116-117, 120-121, 146-147, 148-149, 152-153, 154-155, 164-165
TRILLIUM; 156-157
Trust; 50-51, 130-131
Trusting; 172-173

U

Unique Design; 148-149

V

VINE; 158-159

W

W.D. Davies; 72-73
Wait; 50-51, 78-79, 86-87, 122-123, 140-141, 172-173
Waiting On God; 172-173

Walk; 42-43, 60-61, 82-83, 100-101
Warmth; 12-13
Watch; 72-73
WATER(S); 40-41, 44-45, 46-47, 82-83, 100-101, 102-103, 110-111, 136-137, 160-161, 162-163, 166-167, 174-175
WATERFALL(S); 164-165
Watering; 100-101
WEB; 128-129
WEED; 150-151
WELL; 166-167
WHEEL; 84-85
WHIRLWIND; 16-17
Whisper(ing); 78-79
Wild; 168-169
WILDERNESS; 168-169
WILDFLOWERS; 170-171
WILDLIFE; 70-71, 172-173

William Blake; 144-145
WIND; 78-79, 174-175
WINDS; 168-169
WINGS; 22-23, 68-69
Winnebago Indian Prayer; 144-145
WOLVES; 76-77
Women's Uncommon Prayers; 120-121
Wonder; 48-49
Wood, Douglas; 92-93
WOOD(S); 70-71, 72-73, 86-87, 114-115, 116-117
Worries; 126-127
Wright, Alan; 132-133

Y
Yoruba Poem; 42-43

Z

COPYRIGHTS

Credits/Permissions

Acorn, pages 12-13
by Lyman Abbott, *Leaves of Gold*, 1948, published by Brownlow.

All Things Bright and Beautiful, pages 14-15
Cecil F. Alexander, *Hymns for Little Children*, 1848

Birds, pages 18-19
Overheard in an Orchard by Annie Elizabeth Cheney, 1917

Birds, pages 20-21
Scott Hoezee, *Remember Creation: God's World of Wonder and Delight*,
Grand Rapids MI: William B. Eerdmans Publ. Co. 1998, pg 52

Soaring, pages 22-23
From *Concerning the Nature of Things*, Sir William Bragg. From
DVD, *Extraordinary Visions! With Dewitt Jones*, Dewitt Jones
Productions, www.DewittJones.com

Birdsong, pages 24-25
Brief quote from "Making Peace" (on pp. 31-2) from HIGH TIDE
IN TUCSON: ESSAYS FROM NOW OR NEVER by Barbara
Kingsolver, Copyright (c) 1995 by Barbara Kingsolver. Reprinted by
permission of HarperCollins Publishers.

Cemetery/Graveyard, pages 30-31
"I NEVER WANTED TO BE BORN" by John L. Bell Copyright
© 1995, Wild Goose Resource Group, Iona Community, Scotland,
GIA Publications, Inc, exclusive North American agent 7404 S.
Mason Ave., Chicago, IL 60638 www.giamusic.com 800.442.1358
All rights reserved. Used by permission.

Crows, pages 36-37
By Thomas Merton from NEW SEEDS OF CONTEMPLATION,
copyright © 1961 by The Abbey of Gethsemani, Inc. Reprinted by
permission of New Directions Publishing Corp.

Mushroom, pages 84-85
© 1995 Henri Nouwen and reprinted by permission from *Leadership* journal. www.leadershipjournal.net
Nature, pages 86-87
John Burroughs *The Gospel of Nature,* 1912

Nearness of God, pages 88-89
Praise to You…from whom the evening flows by Elyse Frishman, *This is an hour of change* adapted from Leah Goldberg, translated by Bernard Mehlman, *Where Might I find You* translated by Joel and Larry Hoffman are from the prayer book *Mishkan T'filah: A Reform Siddur,* and are under the copyright protection of the Central Conference of American Rabbis and reprinted for one time use by permission of the CCAR. All rights reserved.

Nuts, pages 90-91
Julian of Norwich (1342-1416)

Pine Tree, pages 92-93
From *Of Earth and Sky, "Paddle Whispers,"* by Douglas Wood, University of Minnesota Press. Used with permission.

Pit-Hole, pages 94-95
From David James Duncan, OrionMagazine.org

Rainbow, pages 104-105
IONA, A Pilgrim's Guide by Jan Sutch Pickard, Canterbury Press Norwich St. Mary's Works, St. Mary's Plain Norwich, Norfolk (UK) NR3 3BH ISBN 978-1-85311-810-4

Rain, pages 102-103
By Thomas Merton, from RAIDS ON THE UNSPEAKABLE, copyright © 1966 by The Abbey of Gethsemani, Inc. Reprinted by permission of New Directions Publishing Corp.

Redbush, pages 106-107
Browning, Elizabeth Barrett, 1857

Reservoir, pages 110-111
From *Sermons on the Song of Songs* by Bernard of Clairvaux (1090-1153)

River, pages 112-113
Thanks to Renni Morris in TN for sharing this idea.

Longing for God: Seven Paths of Christian Devotion by Richard J. Foster and Gayle D. Beebe, InterVarsity Press, 2009.

This is My Father's World, pages 144-145
This is My Father's World, by Maltbie D. Babcock, 1901

Tree, pages 146-147
By Thomas Merton from NEW SEEDS OF CONTEMPLATION, copyright © 1961 by The Abbey of Gethsemani, Inc. Reprinted by permission of New Directions Publishing Corp.

Trees, pages 154-155
Sharing Nature with Children, by Joseph Cornell, Dawn Publications, 1998 p. 29. Used with permission.
Water, pages 160-161
Amy Charmichael, *His Thoughts Said...His Father Said* (Fort Washington, PA: CLC Publications, 1941, 1979), p. 64. Used with permission.

Waterfall, pages 164-165
First published in John J. Deeney (ed.), *A Golden Treasury of Chinese Poetry* (Research Centre for Translation, The Chinese University of Hong Kong, 1989), p. 29. Reprinted by permission of the Research Centre for Translation, The Chinese University of Hong Kong.

Well-Spring, pages 166-167
Rita Minehan, *Rekindling the Flame: A Pilgrimage in the Footsteps of Brigid of Kildare*, Solas Bhride Community, 1999, page 35. Used with permission.

Wilderness, pages 168-169
Sand County Almanac and Sketches Here and There by Leopold Aldo (1968). By permission of Oxford University Press, Inc. Used with permission.

Wildlife, pages 172-173
From *Waiting on God*, by Andrew Murray.

Scripture Quotations

THE PILGRIMAGE CONTINUES...

Even as this book goes to press, we are discovering new gifts in nature. There will be a second book, *Pilgrim Walk at the Sea,* to be published in 2012 and a third, *Pilgrim Walk in the City,* to be published in 2013.

We'd love to hear from you. If you make an interesting discovery, send us your reflection and we might include it in one of the upcoming books, or a future edition of *Pilgrim Walk in the Woods.* Send submissions to submissions@pilgrimwalk.com.

If you have enjoyed this book, additional copies may be purchased for friends at www.HolyPaths.org.

All proceeds go to Holy Paths, Inc, a 501c3 non-profit committed to supporting communities of faith in their journey toward wholeness and intimacy with God.

Susanne Hassell provides spiritual direction, an ancient discipline that involves careful listening and guidance for growing in faith. Holy Paths hosts contemplative retreats designed to provide rest from the demands of life and space to hear how God is leading. For more information, visit www.HolyPaths.org.

Holy Paths

GUIDANCE | COMPANIONSHIP | REST